RUPERT BROOKE:
THE COLLECTED POEMS

From a photograph by Sherril Schell

Rupert Brooke

1913

RUPERT BROOKE:
THE COLLECTED POEMS

WITH A MEMOIR BY
EDWARD MARSH

Introduction by
Gavin Ewart

SIDGWICK & JACKSON
LONDON

First published July 1918; Sixteen Impressions
2nd Edition Revised November 1928; Seven Impressions
3rd Edition Revised November 1942; Sixteen Impressions
4th Edition Revised February 1987

Introduction copyright © 1987 by Gavin Ewart

Printed in Great Britain by
Anchor Brendon Ltd
for Sidgwick & Jackson Ltd
1 Tavistock Chambers, Bloomsbury Way
London WC2A 2SJ

ISBN 0–283–99449–5 (Cased)
ISBN 0–283–99453–3 (Limp)

NOTE

The first edition of this book contained the following 'Introduction' by Mrs Brooke and 'Note' by myself:

I feel that an apology is due to those who have been looking for some time for a Memoir of my son. The chief reason for the delay has been my great desire to gain the collaboration of some of his contemporaries at Cambridge and during his young manhood, for I believe strongly that they knew the largest part of him. Up to now it has been found impossible to do this, much as I should have wished it; and as since his death many of them have also laid down their lives, there is no longer any hope of doing so in the future. I have therefore consented to the Memoir coming out now, although it is of necessity incomplete. I cannot speak strongly enough of the ability and loving care that Mr Marsh has given to the work.

M. R. B.

April 1918

This Memoir was written in August 1915, a few months after Rupert Brooke's death, and my intention was to publish it with his collected poems in the course of that year. Circumstances prevented this, and now that three years have passed I ought probably to rewrite it in the changed perspective and on a different scale. As this is impossible for several reasons, I have had to be contented with a general revision, and the

5

NOTE

addition of letters which have since come into my hands.

I am very grateful to his Mother and to those of his friends who have allowed me to quote from his letters and from their accounts of him.

E. M.

April 1918

The poems have hitherto been printed in the reverse of chronological order, for the reason that this was the arrangement chosen by Rupert Brooke for the only volume published in his lifetime. But the better way is to begin at the beginning, and they now appear, as far as possible, in the sequence in which they were written. One poem, *Fafaïa*, which was not available in 1918, has been included in the section called 'The South Seas'; and another, *It's not going to happen again*, has been added to the Appendix. Both these have been published in the *London Mercury*.

EDWARD MARSH

September 1928

CONTENTS

7

CONTENTS

8

CONTENTS

9

CONTENTS

INTRODUCTION

The stereotype of the young, beautiful, tall, blond poet is a very well-established one in our century (Rupert Brooke, Stephen Spender, Andrew Motion). It owes something to the Romantic poets who died young in the 1820s, Keats, Shelley and Byron – although Keats wasn't very tall and Byron wasn't all that young – but most of all it's based on Brooke.

Rupert Brooke has always been a poet very hard to disentangle from his image as a Golden Boy. My own experience with him must have been shared by many. In the late Twenties, when I was in my very early teens, I admired *The Soldier* because I was taught to admire it. This was the only poem by Brooke that was put before me, as far as I can remember. Next, I became disillusioned. Brooke died in an imperialist war, and such a poem glorified it; the poem was also sentimental – why should English air be very much different from any other country's air?

By this time, in 1932 let us say, my interest was in Eliot, Pound, and Auden. I didn't think much of *Grantchester* (which I still consider twee); but I did like Brooke's poems on the more unpleasant subjects: people being sick crossing the Channel, fat men lusting after women at Wagner concerts. These at least proved to me that he wasn't just a patriotic songster. Nowadays, after various re-readings, I think and hope that I have a balanced view.

But the image of the Golden Boy, created for the literati by Edward Marsh's valedictory *Memoir* of 1915, (reprinted here), and for the general public by the Dean of St Paul's quoting a sonnet in his Easter Sermon of that year, and Winston Churchill's letter to *The Times* soon after Brooke's death ('A voice had become audible, a note had been struck, more thrilling, more able to do justice to the nobility of our youth in arms engaged in this present war, than any other,' etc., etc.) is still something that stands between us and the poetry. For, just as it's no good thinking of Kipling as a straight jingo imperialist, it's no good thinking of Brooke as the pure young soldier eager to die for his country.

Luckily, since 1915, when he died his very unheroic death on the Greek island of Scyros – bitten by an insect, he succumbed to blood poisoning before he had seen action of any kind – a good many facts have come to light. He had unhappy love affairs, he was not uniformly admired and successful, he suffered from self-doubt. There was a minor homosexual love affair and a nervous breakdown. The letters of his Bloomsbury friends and other reminiscences combine to give a very much clearer picture. Marsh's *Memoir* is admirable and does give some

INTRODUCTION

idea of what he must have been like; it's particu larly good in that it quotes Brooke's own letters. But it's tinged with sentimentality. The final paragraph, quoted from a letter of Denis Browne, reads: '. . . we passed Rupert's island at sunset. The sea and sky in the East were grey and misty; but it stood out in the West, black and immense, with a crimson glowing halo round it. Every colour had come into the sea and sky to do him honour; and it seemed that the island must ever be shining with his glory that we buried there'.

The best and most complete short account of Brooke's life and work is *Rupert Brooke, His Life and His Legend* by John Lehmann, published in 1980. Brooke inspired strong emotions. Beautiful, witty and charming, he also appeared to Virginia Woolf as 'jealous, moody, ill-balanced', while Leonard Woolf and E.M. Forster thought he had a 'cruel streak' and was 'essentially hard'. People who have as much adulation as he had, do often exhibit these qualities.

The published poems begin in 1905, when Brooke was eighteen. The very early ones are like Matthew Arnold (*Here in the dark, O heart;/ Alone with the enduring Earth, and Night*), like Ernest Dowson (*'Mid youth and song, feasting and carnival,/Through laughter, through the roses, as of old/Comes Death*), like James Elroy Flecker (a matter of rhythms in the various *Songs*), like the Pre-Raphaelites (a lot of Love and Gates and

Golden Stairs), like Swinburne (*The pale Lethean wine within thy chalices!* . . .), like W.E. Henley (*I broke the Night's primeval bars,/I dared the old abysmal curse,/And flashed through ranks of frightened stars/Suddenly on the universe!*). They vary. Some are quite accomplished, others not; or, simply, standard adolescent love poetry (*Touch of your hands* and *smell of your hair!*). Most promising are the chunks of anti-romantic realism – a sonnet about two snoring Germans in a sleeper on a train journey, and the poem *Wagner*, describing a fat sensualist in the Queen's Hall in 1908:

> *Creeps in half wanton, half asleep,*
> * One with a fat wide hairless face.*
> *He likes love-music that is cheap;*
> * Likes women in a crowded place;*
> *   And wants to hear the noise they're making.*

This is certainly one of his best poems, a fifteen-line satire with no weak lines. It's not very 'deep', but it's very effective.

Weak lines in the early verse are not hard to find; nor are bad rhymes – 'mire' rhyming with 'tire' because he couldn't think of anything better (*Into the shade and loneliness and mire/Of the last land!*). A kind of silliness too:

> *And turn, and toss your brown delightful head*
> *Amusedly, among the ancient Dead.*

14

INTRODUCTION

Among the poems of lost love of 1909 and 1910, *Dust* seems one of the best, though weakened by one failed adjective (*your quick hair*). *Kindliness* strays too much in its syntax – one of his faults – but *Mummia* is outstanding (about drinking powdered mummies as an aphrodisiac), an exercise in the John Donne 'metaphysical' style:

> *Drunk on the dead, and medicined*
> *With spiced imperial dust,*
> *In a short night they reeled to find*
> *Ten centuries of lust.*

The Fish (1911) is, one might say, a wet 'dry run' for the great satirical poem *Heaven* that followed two years later; it suffers from Browningism (*Who lips the roots o' the shore*), and love of the unusual word ('hyaline', a Miltonic word for the glassiness of the sea). There's nothing wrong with such words except that they look like showing off – 'crescive', for example, in another poem of the period, and 'immote'. Virginia Woolf has described how he used to leave blanks in his poems until he'd found the right word. Perhaps, sometimes, a word can be too 'right'. In Milton's verse the Latin and Greek words don't look out of place, because his whole vocabulary is like that. In Brooke they give us the feeling that a Georgian nature poet has read too much Andrew Marvell. On the other hand, when he is after simplicity, he can give us bathos:

15

INTRODUCTION

Among the leaves. They shed around me
Calm clouds of scent, that I did weep,
And stroked my face. I fell asleep.

Brooke wrote a lot of sonnets. They are often well–intentioned rather than successful. *The Hill* (1910) is one of the first ones that work. It's very 'young', and a bit fatuous, but it has some force:

Breathless, we flung us on the windy hill,
Laughed in the sun, and kissed the lovely grass.

Like *The Soldier* (*If I should die, think only this of me*) it's too consciously heroic (. . . *Proud we were,/And laughed, that had such brave true things to say*), with a touch of Newbolt about it (*We shall go down with unreluctant tread/Rose-crowned into the darkness!*); yet it has a mild sting in the tail, *–And then you suddenly cried, and turned away.* Does 'cried' mean 'wept', or simply 'cried out'? It's not easy to say.

Housman also has a look–in, in *The One Before The Last* (1910):

Oh! bitter thoughts I had in plenty.
But here's the worst of it–
I shall forget, in Nineteen-twenty,
You ever hurt a bit.

The 'disillusioned' poems, of which there are quite a few, are often crude (*And flaming brains are*

16

INTRODUCTION

the white heart of all) Writing about love is one of
the hardest things a poet can ever set himself to
do. *Menelaus and Helen*, a matching pair of
sonnets, though melodramatic, goes a long way
towards succeeding. Too often it's hard to know
what's happening (*The enormous wheels of will/
Drove me cold-eyed on tired and sleepless feet*). Is he
on a chariot, roller-skates, a treadmill? These
poems often sound impressive, but often they
don't say very much – or what they say is
unclear.

Jealousy, because it's straightforward, is an
exception. It succeeds, because Brooke's hatred
and fear of old age was so genuine. *Song* (*'Oh!
Love', they said, 'is King of Kings'*) is another
comparatively simple love poem, and comparatively successful. *A Channel Passage*, one of the
'unpleasant' poems, makes a telling comparison
between sea-sickness and the memories of a
failed love affair – the experience not, as it were,
digested. The realism (*Old meat, good meals,
brown gobbets, up I throw*) is in its way welcome
after all the woods at dawn, goddesses, winds
and silences, the Hopes, the Dreams, the Sighs.

The last section but one (1911–1914) leads off
with *Grantchester*, a straight comparison in light
verse of a Berlin café with Brooke's Cambridge
retreat. The reference to '*Temperamentvoll* German Jews' now looks a bit racist; but we mustn't
forget that anti-semitism was standard among
the British upper and middle classes at this time.

17

INTRODUCTION

G.K. Chesterton seriously suggested, in an essay, that Jews should be made to wear special clothes – a thought that Hitler later put into practice. Germans were not popular because of their arrogance and the commercial rivalry. *Grantchester*, generally speaking, is *The Scholar Gipsy* touched with silliness – *And spectral dance, before the dawn,/A hundred Vicars down the lawn.* Debased derivatives followed – *That cow resembles a Rural Dean* (a Noel Coward revue song, *Something to do with Spring*) and *Out on the lawn the Cabman dances* (a line by J.B. Morton, a.k.a. *Beachcomber*). 'Little' is a key word (*And little kindly winds that creep, . . . and hear the breeze/ Sobbing in the little trees*), standing for innocence and lack of pretension. But, in spite of the church clock and the honey for tea, this is not a good poem, though it is a famous one.

It's 1912, and Brooke is still using words like 'frore'. *Mary and Gabriel* is an Annunciation, but not very remarkable. *The Chilterns* (1913), on the other hand, another piece of Housmania, is one of his best:

> *And I shall find some girl perhaps,*
> *And a better one than you,*
> *With eyes as wise, but kindlier,*
> *And lips as soft, but true,*
> *And I daresay she will do.*

The Way That Lovers Use also has a pleasant

irony and detachment. *The Funeral Of Youth* is a
'list' poem. He did these well; *The Great Lover* is
the best example (the pleasures of life include *the
rough male kiss of blankets*). The section headed
South Seas has some rather undistinguished love
sonnets (*and wove/Its laughter with the dancing light
o' the spray*), the best being *He Wonders Whether
To Praise Or To Blame Her* and a ballad, *There's
Wisdom in Women*. But it also includes *Heaven*,
the satire on the religious ideas of fishes —
arguably his best poem:

> *Fish say, they have their Stream and Pond;*
> *But is there anything Beyond?*
> *This life cannot be All, they swear,*
> *For how unpleasant, if it were!*

As a piece of comic rhetoric, debunking the
desire for immortality, it has no faults. A runner-
up, of a different kind, is the Marvell-like *Tiare
Tahiti* – his best South Seas poem, where the
wished-for after-life is an extension of the Tahiti
happiness:

> *With lips that fade, and human laughter*
> *And faces individual,*
> *Well this side of Paradise! . . .*
> *There's little comfort in the wise.*

The six sonnets grouped under the heading
1914, his last poems, are full of fine feelings,

perhaps too full of them. *The Soldier* is the best written (and the most famous), with its repeated references to 'England' – which, for an Englishman at least, underlines the emotion. The most unthinking is *Peace*:

Now, God be thanked Who has matched us with His
*   hour,*
*   And caught our youth, and wakened us from*
*   sleeping,*
With hand made sure, clear eye, and sharpened power,
*   To turn, as swimmers into cleanness leaping,*
Glad from a world grown old and cold and weary

Of course in 1914 he wasn't to know that those swimmers were about to leap, not into 'cleanness', but into the mud and blood of trench warfare on the Western Front. His parting shots at, *the sick hearts that honour could not move,/And half-men, and their dirty songs and dreary,/And all the little emptiness of love!* were inspired by his quarrels with the Bloomsbury intellectuals such as Lytton Strachey, and his unhappy love affair with Ka Cox. Instead of trying to untangle the Gordian knot of life's difficulties, you cut it with the sword of war.

The two sonnets called *The Dead* are attempts to justify the slaughter of young men by calling it noble (*And Nobleness walks in our ways again;/And we have come into our heritage*). The second of them is less hysterical – another 'list' poem, cataloguing the experiences of life that the dead have forfeited. The sestet is a very beautiful image of frost (death) immobilising the water (active life).

Even at the time Brooke's fellow-poet Charles Sorley, eight years younger, wrote: 'He is far too obsessed with his own sacrifice, regarding the going to war of himself (and others) as a highly intense, remarkable and sacrificial exploit, whereas it is merely the conduct demanded of him (and others) by the turn of circumstances, where non-compliance with this demand would have made life intolerable . . . he has clothed his attitude in fine words: but he has taken the sentimental attitude.'

Brooke, after all, was a socialist; he should have recognised a capitalist commercial war when he saw one. He could have been a pacifist, like Bertrand Russell and other Cambridge intellectuals, although this would have demanded a courage he didn't possess. Instead he opted for heroics, tempted by his own special position – with the grand dinners, the house-parties, Eddie Marsh in love with him, the talks with Churchill in the Admiralty, the literary acclaim. It's easy to make a moral judgement; but nobody then foresaw the bloodiness of the fighting, the stupidity of the generals, even that the war would last four years. Brooke was a remarkable and very talented man; he worked very hard at his craft – we have Virginia Woolf's word for this –

taking poetry very seriously indeed. If he veered too far towards 'the glamorous-romantic-vague' (Leavis' later charge against Stephen Spender), we must remember that this was the fashion of his day. The long adolescence of Rugby and King's sealed him off from most of the realities of ordinary life.

Brooke, in contrast to the high-and-mighty dramatics of a lot of his verse, did have a talent for a rather embittered kind of light piece; two of the earlier but later-printed poems *Sonnet Reversed* and *It's Not Going To Happen Again* show this. And one fragment (*I strayed about the deck, an hour, to-night*) of April 1915 shows that he could write more realistically of his fellow servicemen, when he wasn't spotlighting them too intensely as heroes.

What kind of poems would he have written if he had survived the war? It's impossible to say. Very much better ones, would be my guess; after he had survived the first patriotic enthusiasm, the war poems themselves would certainly have changed. Satire would almost certainly have replaced the romanticism.

As it is, we have a handful of very good poems – should we say ten? – and many others that are very enjoyable though immature, a young man's poems. Of these, the war sonnets are part of literary history, whatever their virtues or short-comings. The 'unheroic' poems, too, are an attempt to write 'modern' verse; Brooke never

INTRODUCTION

loaded his poems with archaisms or inversions (*To you I go*, etc.) in the way that the less talented Georgians did. Although he's not untainted by poetic diction, as the conventional poets of his day understood it, he doesn't wallow in it. There aren't any 'Tis'es, 'Twas'es or Wheresoe'ers, though he does have 'Mid and 'Twixt.

At his best, he could write clearly and effectively — a poem that is technically perfect, good all through (*Heaven* is the best example). Indeed *Heaven*, if the word means anything, could be considered a 'great' poem. It's not quite up there with Marvell's *To His Coy Mistress*, which, in its tone of playful exaggeration, it slightly resembles, but it's not far short. It does for false religion (the kind that's only interested in personal immortality) exactly what Marvell sets out to do for sexual flirtatiousness and regard for reputation.

Rupert Brooke never got his life sorted out (this doesn't matter as far as poetry is concerned). The really sad thing, for us, is that he died with so much unwritten, and such infinite promise, at the age of only twenty-eight

Gavin Ewart, 1987

I

RUPERT BROOKE was born at Rugby on August 3rd, 1887. His father was William Parker Brooke, a Rugby master, son of Canon Brooke of Bath; and his mother was Mary Ruth Cotterill. He was the second of three brothers.[1]

When he was five years old his father became Housemaster of School Field, which was his home till 1910. He loved the house and the garden, especially his own particular long grass-path with borders and pergolas, where he used to walk up and down reading. At this House he entered Rugby in 1901, from the preparatory school at Hillbrow, and next year won a scholarship.

His school life was very happy. In his first year at Cambridge, reading out a paper on Modern Poetry which he had written at the end of his last term at Rugby for the School Society called Ἔρανος, and afraid that the alarming undergraduates might think it sentimental, he excused himself by explaining the circumstances in which he wrote it. 'I had been happier at Rugby,' he said, 'than I can find words to say. As I looked back at five years, I seemed to see almost every hour golden and radiant, and always increasing in beauty as I grew more conscious; and I could not (and cannot) hope for or even quite imagine such

[1] Dick, who was six years older, died in 1907; and Alfred, three years younger, was killed near Vermelles in June 1915, serving as a lieutenant in the Post Office Rifles.

happiness elsewhere. And then I found the last days of all this slipping by me, and with them the faces and places and life I loved, and I without power to stay them. I became for the first time conscious of transcience, and parting, and a great many other things.'

This happiness was compounded from many sources: friendship, games (he played for the School in both the XI and the XV), and books. He was a balanced combination of the athletic and the intellectual types of schoolboy—'always with a ball in his hand and a book in his pocket' is a vivid little description. 'Rupert' (writes a contemporary in the VIth who was at another house, and afterwards became an Assistant Master[1]), 'first of all people at school gave me an inkling of what a full life really meant. I was an awful Philistine, and still am, I fear; but he, with no appearance of superiority or attempt at preaching, as keen as any of us on all the immensely important events in school life, and always ready for a rag, impressed us as no one else could with the fact that these things were not all—not even the most important. And the best thing about him was that he was not out to impress us—it was just being himself.'

His great school-friend Hugh Russell-Smith, since killed in action, wrote in the Rugby paper, *The Meteor*, when he died:

'For the first two or three years, I think, few of us realised that someone out of the ordinary had come

[1] Hubert Podmore, who, before he was killed in action, gave Mrs Brooke leave to publish this extract from his letter to her.

among us. He was rather shy and quiet, though he at
once proved himself a good athlete, and he lived much
the same life as anyone else. Gradually, however, we
began to notice little things about him. Instead of
coming "down town" with us, he used to go off to
the Temple Library to read the reviews of books in
the *Morning Post* and *Chronicle*. He read Walter Pater,
and authors we knew very little about. He read a good
deal of poetry, and he let us find him in raptures over
Swinburne. He began to wear his hair rather longer
than other people. Still, he played games enthusiastically, and helped us to become Cock House in football and in cricket. Gradually most of us in the House
came under his spell. We accepted his literary interests.
He was so straightforward and unaffected and natural
about them, and he took our chaff so well, that we
couldn't have helped doing so. Perhaps they amused
most of us, but one or two—and those the most un-
likely—were occasionally found clumsily trying to
see what there really was in such things. But it was his
personal charm that attracted us most, his very simple
and lovable nature. Few could resist it. When in his
last year he became head of the House, almost everyone came under the sway of his personality. It seems
to me now, as it seemed then, that there really was a
spirit in School Field which made it rather different
from any other House. It was due, I believe, partly to
Rupert, partly to his father. The situation might have
been difficult for both. The way in which things
actually turned out shows one of the most delightful
sides of Rupert. He was in all things more than loyal

to his father, but he never made it awkward for the rest of us. His sense of fun saw him through, and it helped us a good deal to know that he would not misinterpret all the little pleasantries that boys make at the expense of their Housemaster. The result was a sort of union between the Housemaster and the House, which made very much for good.

'Outside the House, his worth was realised to the full by some—by the Upper Bench, and by a few of the Masters who knew and loved him. He rose to a high place in the VIth, won two prizes for his poems, played cricket and football for the School, and became a Cadet Officer in the Corps. But I think he was never a School hero. It was chiefly his House that knew his lovableness. And when he was at Cambridge, I think he always loved the House lunches, which we used to have nearly every week. The last letter I had from him was one in which he was talking of members of the House who had fallen in the war.

'Rupert had an extraordinary vitality at school, which showed itself in a glorious enthusiasm and an almost boisterous sense of fun—qualities that are only too rare in combination. Of his enthusiasm it is hard to speak; we knew less about it, although we felt it. We knew much more of his glorious fooling—in his letters, in his inimitable and always kind burlesques of masters or boys, in his parodies of himself. He seemed almost always ready for laughter. It is often the small things that stand out most vividly in one's mind. I see Rupert singing at the very top of his

voice, with a magnificent disregard for tune, the
evening hymn we used to have so often at Bigside
Prayers. I see him rushing on to the Close to release a
sheep that had become entangled in one of the nets. I
see him tearing across the grass so as not to be late for
Chapel. I generally think of him with a book. He had
not yet developed that love of the country and that
passion for swimming with which the friends of his
Grantchester days associate him. He used to read,
when we used to walk or bathe. But whatever he was
doing or wherever he was, he was always the same
incomparable friend. He has often quoted to me a
verse of Hilaire Belloc:

> *From quiet homes and first beginning,*
> *Out to the undiscovered ends,*
> *There's nothing worth the wear of winning,*
> *But laughter and the love of friends.*

How much Rupert loved Rugby while he was there,
I know; and I know too how much those who knew
him there loved him.'

The letters which he wrote in his last year at school
are radiant. 'I am enjoying everything immensely at
present. To be among 500 people, all young and
laughing, is intensely delightful and interesting. . . .[1]
I am seated on the topmost pinnacle of the Temple of
Joy. Wonderful things are happening all around me.
Some day when all the characters are dead—they are

[1] Throughout this book, three dots mean that there are dots
in the original letters; six, that something is omitted. Most of
the Rugby letters quoted were from St John Lucas.

sure to die young—I shall put it all in a book. I am
in the midst of a beautiful comedy—with a sense of
latent tears—and the dramatic situations work out
delightfully. The rest are only actors; I am actor and
spectator as well, and I delight in contriving effective
exits. The world is of gold and ivory. . . . How is London? Here the slushy roads, grey skies, and epidemic
mumps cannot conceal a wonderful beauty in the air
which makes New Big School almost bearable.' And
in the summer: 'I am infinitely happy. I am writing
nothing. I am content to live. After this term is over,
the world awaits. But I do not now care what will
come then. Only, my present happiness is so great
that I fear the jealous gods will requite me afterwards with some terrible punishment, death perhaps –
or life.'

'Work' was only one of the lesser elements which
went to make up all this joy. He got a fair number of
prizes, and went to King's with a scholarship: but
lessons seem to have been almost the only thing he
didn't as a rule care for. He would have liked to read
the books as books, but grammar irked him. When he
came to 'extra work' for the scholarship examination,
he enjoyed it. 'This introduces me to many authors
whom the usual course neglects as "unclassical.". . .
Theocritus almost compensates me for all the inter-
minable dullness of Demosthenes and the grammars
on other days. I never read him before. I am wildly,
madly enchanted by him.' He never became an accu-
rate scholar, and though he enjoyed certain authors,
and had a special love for Plato, I don't think Greek

and Latin played the part in his development which might have been expected.

His voluntary reading, at school and afterwards, was mainly English—quantities of prose, but still more poetry, in which his taste was very comprehensive; and his zealous interest in contemporary work had already begun. A paper on Modern Poetry, which he read to the Ἔρανος Society, presses on his hearers Kipling, Henley, Watson, Yeats, A. E., and —— Ernest Dowson. This brings us to his amusing phase of 'decadence.' From 1905 till well into his second year at Cambridge he entertained a *culte* (in such intensity, somewhat belated) for the literature that is now called 'ninety-ish'— Pater,[1] Wilde, and Dowson. This was a genuine enthusiasm, as anyone may see from his earliest published work, especially the poems written in the alexandrine of *Cynara*, of which the 'Day that I have loved' is the culmination. But he loved to make fun of it, and of himself in it; for all through his life his irony played first on himself. Here is the setting of

[1] A little parody with which he won a *Westminster Gazette* prize in 1907 may be worth preserving here: '*From "Marius the Bank Clerk," by Walter Pater (Book II, Chap. ix, "Procrastination"*). Well! it was there, as he beat upon the station gate (that so symbolic barrier!) and watched the receding train, that the idea came upon him; casting, as it were, a veil of annoyance over the vague melancholy of his features; and filling, not without a certain sedate charm, as of a well-known ritual, his mind with a now familiar sense of loss—a very *desiderium*—a sense only momentarily perceptible, perhaps, among the other emotions and thoughts, that swarmed, like silver doves, about his brain.'

a dialogue: 'The Close in a purple evening in June. The air is full of the sound of cricket and the odour of the sunset. On a green bank *Rupert* is lying. There is a mauve cushion beneath his head, and in his hand E. Dowson's collected poems, bound in pale sorrowful green. He is clothed in indolence and flannels. *Enter Arthur.* "Good-morrow," says *Arthur*. "What a tremulous sunset!"' But that is all he is allowed to say. *Rupert* proceeds with an elaborately 'jewelled' harangue, ending 'I thank you for this conversation. You talk wonderfully. I love listening to epigrams. I wonder if the dead still delight in epigrams. I love to think of myself seated on the greyness of Lethe's banks, and showering ghosts of epigrams and shadowy paradoxes upon the assembled wan-eyed dead. We shall smile, a little wearily I think, remembering. . . . Farewell.' 'Farewell,' says poor *Arthur*, opening his mouth for the second time—and *exit*.

'I am busy with an enormous romance, of which I have written five chapters. It begins with my famous simile[1] about the moon, but soon gets much more lewd. One of the chief characters is a dropsical leper whose limbs and features have been absorbed in one vast soft paunch. He looks like a great human slug, and he croaks infamous little songs from a wee round mouth with yellow lips. The others are less respectable.

'Did you see the bowdlerised decadent?[2] I suppose

[1] This was as follows: 'The moon was like an enormous yellow scab on the livid flesh of some leper.'
[2] *Nero* at His Majesty's Theatre.

the scenery looked extremely valuable. I dare not witness it. Nero is one of the few illusions I have left. All my others are departing one by one. I read a book recently which proved that Apollo was an aged Chieftain who lived in Afghanistan and had four wives and cancer in the stomach; and the other day I found myself—my last hope?—acting on moral principles.'

'This morning I woke with ophthalmia,' he wrote in another letter, 'one of the many diseases raging through Rugby. It is all owing to a divine mistake. I wanted to get rose-rash, being both attracted by the name and desirous to have the disease over before the time of the Italian "tour" came. Therefore yestre'en I prayed to Æsculapius a beautiful prayer in Sapphics —it began, I think, ἵμερος νῦν ἐστὶ ῥόδοις πυρέττειν, . . . but either my Greek was unintelligible, or the names of ills have changed since Æsculapius, for I awoke and found the God had sent me this, the least roseate of diseases.'

He wished, of course, or rather wished to be thought to wish, to shock and astonish the respectable; but he did not in practice go very far in that direction. His hair, slightly longer than usual, has already been mentioned. Ties might not be coloured; but there was no rule against their being 'puff' and made of *crêpe de chine*; and such ties he wore, as did the other school swells. It was amusing to cause a flutter in the orthodox School Societies, of which he was really an active and enthusiastic member, though one might not think so from his accounts of their proceedings. 'Last Sunday I read a little paper on *Atalanta*, and was mightily pleased. The usual papers we have on such subjects as Hood or Calverley—"something to make you laugh.". . . I saw my opportunity, and took it. "Have I not," I said, "many a time and oft been bored beyond endurance by such Philistines? Now my revenge comes; I shall be merciless!" So I prepared a very long and profound paper, full of beautiful quotations, and read it to them for a long time, and they were greatly bored. They sat round in chairs and slumbered uneasily, moaning a little; while I in the centre ranted fragments of choruses and hurled epithets upon them. At length I ended with Meleager's last speech, and my voice was almost husky with tears; so that they awoke, and wondered greatly, and sat up, and yawned, and entered into a discussion on *Tragedy*, wherein I advanced the most wild and heterodox and antinomian theories, and was very properly squashed. So, you see, even in Rugby the Philistines don't get it their own way always.'

'I am finishing my paper on James Thomson.[1] I have cut out all the wicked parts, but I still fear for the reception. Last week we had a paper on T. Gray. The stupendous ass who wrote and read it, after referring to the Elegy as "a fine lyric," ended with the following incomparable words: "In conclusion, we may give Gray a place among the greatest, above all, except perhaps Shakespeare, Milton, and Tennyson." This lewd remark roused me from the carefully-

[1] He had 'ransacked the eight bookshops in Charing Cross Road' for Thomson's works. (This is, of course, the author of *The City of Dreadful Night*, not of *The Seasons*.)

34

studied pose of irritating and sublime nonchalance which I assume on such occasions. I arose, and made acid and quite unfair criticisms of Gray and Tennyson, to the concealed delight of all the avowed Philistines there, and the open disgust of the professing "lovers of literature." I was nearly slain.'

He wrote quantities of poetry at Rugby, a very little of which he thought worth preserving in the '1905–1908' section of his first book. Some of it appeared in the *Phœnix*, a free-lance school paper of which he was twin-editor, and some in the *Venture*, which succeeded the *Phœnix*. His verse of this time shows a good ear, and a love of 'beautiful' words, but not much else. A good deal of it was written when he ought to have been otherwise employed. 'I shall sit in a gondola,' he wrote when he was going to Venice in April 1906, 'and pour forth satires in heroic verse, or moral diatribes in blank verse. Intense surroundings always move me to write in an opposite vein. I gaze on the New Big School, and give utterance to frail diaphanous lyrics, sudden and beautiful as a rose-petal. And when I do an hour's "work" with the Headmaster, I fill notebooks with erotic terrible fragments at which even Sappho would have blushed and trembled.'

In 1904 he was given an extra prize for a poem on *The Pyramids*, and next year he won the real prize with one on *The Bastille*, which he recited on June 24th. 'The speeches were rather amusing. I am informed that my effort was one of the only two audible; and as the other was in a foreign tongue, I carried off the honours. I am also told—by a cricketer friend of mine—that half the audience were moved to laughter, the other half to tears, which I regard as a compliment, though I can understand the feelings of neither half. Anyhow I got a Browning and a Rossetti out of it, which is something, though they *are* in prize-binding.'

Next year he had to fall back on prose. 'I have undertaken to write an Essay for a prize. If I win this I shall stand up next Speech Day and recite weird "historical" platitudes to a vast slumbrous audience. The idea is so pleasingly incongruous that I desire to realise it. Moreover, I once airily told a pedantic and aged man that if I liked I could understand even History, and he, scoffing, stirred my pride to prove it. Therefore I am going to write an Essay on "The Influence of William III on England." Of William III I know very little. He was a King, or something, they say, of the time of Congreve and Wycherley. Of England I know nothing. I thought you might aid me in a little matter like this. If ever you have written an epic, a monograph, an anthology, or a lyric on William III please send it to me that I may quote it in full.' He won the prize (the King's Medal for Prose); and as he got into the XI at about the same time, he left Rugby with honours thick upon him.

II

His first year at King's (1906–7) was rather unsatisfactory. He regretted Rugby; and he was (as always) rather shy, and (for the first and only time) a little on the defensive with the strange people. The 'decadent' pose lingered; he had Aubrey Beardsleys in his room, sat up very late, and didn't get up in the morning. He thought it right to live entirely for the things of the mind; his passion for the country had not yet begun, and it seemed to him a wicked waste of time to walk or swim—two things which came soon afterwards to give him as much pleasure as anything in the world.

His letters are plaintive: 'This place is rather funny to watch; and a little wearying. . . . . . At certain moments I perceive a pleasant kind of peace in the grey ancient walls and green lawns among which I live; a quietude that doesn't compensate for the things I have loved and left, but at times softens their outlines a little. If only I were a poet, I should love such a life very greatly, "remembering moments of passion in tranquillity"; but being first and chiefly only a boy, I am restless and unable to read or write. . . . . . . These people are often clever, and always wearying. The only persons I ever make any effort to see are two who came up with me from my House at Rugby. Here across the Styx we wander about together and talk of the upper world, and sometimes pretend we are children again.'

He joined the A.D.C., and played *Stingo* in *She*

Stoops to Conquer; but his chief public appearance in his first term was in the Greek play, the *Eumenides*. 'The idea of my playing Hermes fell through,' he wrote to his Mother, 'but they have given me the equally large part of the Herald. I stand in the middle of the stage and pretend to blow a trumpet, while somebody in the wings makes a sudden noise. The part is not difficult.' 'I wear a red wig and cardboard armour,' he wrote in another letter, 'and luckily am only visible for a minute.' It turned out that he was one of the successes of the evening. His radiant, youthful figure in gold and vivid red and blue, like a Page in the Riccardi Chapel, stood strangely out against the stuffy decorations and dresses which pervaded those somewhat palmy days of the Cambridge Theatre. After eleven years, the impression has not faded.

At the beginning of next term his elder brother died suddenly. They were very fond of each other, and this was, I suppose, his first great sorrow. 'It seems so strange that you haven't heard', he wrote. 'I had thought that all the world must know. I suppose I ought to have written and told you; but there were so many letters to write; and I had to try to comfort Mother a little. Dick died on Sunday the 13th after a week's illness. Father was with him—but I don't think details matter much. . . . . . . I came up here on Tuesday, partly to escape my Rugby school-friends, and partly that I might be alone.'

'I'm rather wretched and ill,' he writes a little later. 'In my "literary life" I have taken the last step of

38

infamy, and become—a reviewer ! I've undertaken to "do" great slabs of minor poetry for the *Cambridge Review*. I've read volumes of them, all the same, and all exactly the stuff *I* write. I often wonder whether I haven't written several of them myself under a pseudonym, and forgotten about it.'

In his first Long Vacation,[1] 'I work hundreds of hours a day,' he writes, 'at stuffy classics, and ooze with grammar. To save my soul, I write thousands of poems in the evening, and burn them. I'll quote to you one verse of an immensely long one in six cantos, entitled "A Song Illustrative of a Sense of Incompatibility between Self and Universe ; also In Favour of Decease."

> '*Things are beasts,*
>   *Alas! and Alack!*
> *If life is a succession of choreic anapæsts,*
> *When, ah! when shall we arrive at the Parœmiac?*'

Part of this Long was spent at Lulworth, where he wrote to his Mother: 'One day we were reading on the rocks, and I had a Keats in my pocket, and it slipped out, and, falling into a swift current, was borne out to sea. So we leapt into a boat and rowed up and down the coast till we espied it off some rocks. But the sea was rather rough and we could not land on that rocky part, or get near Keats. So we landed half

[1] I may as well mention that I first met him just after the end of the May Term this year. After this I saw him at intervals, and we knew each other pretty well by the summer of 1909.

a mile off on a beach, and came over the rocks to the Keats; and when we found it, I stripped and went in after it and got it. It is indeed quite spoilt; but it only cost two shillings to begin with.' (He did not know at this time of an association which he discovered four years afterwards. 'Oh, I've read Keats,' he writes in 1911, 'and found the most AMAZING thing. The last place he was in was Lulworth. His ship was becalmed outside. He and Severn went ashore and clambered about the rocks all day—his last fairly happy day. He went aboard and wrote, that evening, his last poem—that sonnet. The ship took him on to Italy, coughing blood and suffering Hell because he wouldn't see Fanny any more. Fanny sat in Hampstead, with Mr Brown. It was at the end of Sept. 1820 . . .')

There is a gloomy letter of the day after his birthday, when he became twenty. 'I am now in the depths of despondency because of my age. I'm filled with an hysterical despair to think of fifty dull years more. I hate myself and everyone. I've written almost no verse for ages; and shall never write any more. I've forgotten all rhythm and metre. The words "anapæstic dimeter acatalectic," that fired me once, now leave me cold. The sunset or a child's face no longer reminds me of a bucolic cæsura. But I still read plaintively, to pass the time.' And he can still write at the end of this Long: 'Go back to Cambridge for my second year and laugh and talk with those old dull people on that airless plain! The thought fills me with hideous *ennui*.'

But this mood was already something of a literary

survival, and well understood to be so by his friends.
He went back to games, especially football; and
by the beginning of his second year he had become
one of the most interested and interesting people at
Cambridge.

A young Apollo, golden-haired,
  Stands dreaming on the verge of strife,
Magnificently unprepared
  For the long littleness of life.

Mrs Cornford's epigram on him is well known, but
one could not write about his great days at Cambridge without quoting it—bitter though the irony of
'long' has now become.

Henceforward friends and avocations crowded on
him. He had been the chief advocate of the Labour
Party at Rugby; and at King's he joined various
societies, political and intellectual, mostly more or
less revolutionary—the University Fabian Society, of
which he became President for the year 1909-10; the
Carbonari; and the Heretics. He also belonged to that
old, great, secret, but vaguely famous Brotherhood
from which the membership of Tennyson and others
of the illustrious has lifted a corner of the veil. J. T.
Sheppard, Fellow of King's, gives an account of some
among these activities. 'The Carbonari, I think, he
founded; a Society which, in spite of its terrifying
name, was very friendly. The paper and the talk
which followed it at the one meeting to which, as an
elderly person, I was allowed admission, were frank
and amusing, but my chief memory is of the cheerful

kindliness of the members. Then there were the Fabians, whom he sometimes entertained to a frugal supper of bread and cheese and beer in his rooms, and to whom he never tired of teaching the importance of poets and artists in the good society which is to be built up by our children. His advice to the State was very practical. Since poets and artists matter, and since they need time for development, we, who are not the poets and the artists, ought to organise the material requisites, bread and cheese and leisure, for those who seem to show the promise of good work. He believed that you do not improve a poet by starving and neglecting him; and one good way of showing that we remember him would be to remember also that it is our duty to buy as well as read the works of the poets who are still writing.'

Rupert indeed wore his Socialism with a difference, which comes out in a letter of December 1907, thanking his uncle, Mr Clement Cotterill, for his book, *Human Justice for those at the Bottom*, in which he says that he has been urging his Socialist friends at Cambridge, especially the Fabians, to take a more human view of things. 'Socialism is making great advances at Oxford and Cambridge just now; but its upholders are too apt to make it seem, to others and to themselves, a selfish scheme of economics. They confound the means with the end; and think that a Compulsory Living Wage is the end, instead of a good beginning. Bernard Shaw came down last term, and made a speech that was enthusiastically received, in which he advised a state of things in which each "class" had its own party in Parliament fighting for its own hand. The whole thing was based on selfishness. It was not inspiring.

'Of course they're really sincere, energetic, useful people, and they do a lot of good work. But, as I've said, they're rather hard. Must every cause lose part of its ideal, as it becomes successful? And also they are rather intolerant, especially towards the old order. They sometimes seem to take it for granted that all rich men, and all Conservatives (and most ordinary Liberals) are heartless villains. I have already, thanks, in part, to some words of yours, got some faith in the real, sometimes overgrown, goodness of all men; and that is why I have found your book so good, as a confirmation rather than a revelation. And this faith I have tried to hammer into those Socialists of my generation whom I have come across. But it's sometimes hard. The prejudices of the clever are harder to kill than those of the dull. Also I sometimes wonder whether this Commercialism, or Competition, or whatever the filthy infection is, hasn't spread almost too far, and whether the best hope isn't in some kind of upheaval.'

All this is supplemented in an account written by Hugh Dalton, an intimate friend of this time. 'During our years at Cambridge, Fabianism was at its high tide, and attracted most of those who had any social enthusiasm worth speaking of. Rupert joined the C.U.F.S. in April 1907. He came to me, I remember, and said, "I'm not your sort of Socialist; I'm a William Morris sort of Socialist, but I want to join your

Society as an Associate." He became a full member a
year later. Like many of us, he was falling by then
under the subtle influence of the Webbs, and simul-
taneously the atmosphere of Cambridge was teaching
him to value and to cultivate lucidity of thought and
precision of reasoning. He soon saw the intellectual
limitations of a "William Morris sort of Socialist,"
and though he never studied the fine points of economics, he came to talk very good sense on the larger
economic questions.

'It was through the meetings of the Carbonari that
I first came to know him well. This was a society of
our contemporaries in King's, about a dozen, which
we formed in our first term for papers and discussions.
Rupert and I and one or two others were generally
the last to separate, and sometimes the dawn was in
the sky before we got to bed. We walked round the
Courts and beside the river for hours, trying to get
things clear. For we wanted, half passionately and half
humorously, to get everything clear quickly. Hitherto,
we thought, we had been too young to think, and
soon we might be too busy, and ultimately we should
be too old. The golden time was now.

' "There are only three things in the world," he said
once, vehemently answering some Carbonaro who
had been talking like a Philistine, "one is to read
poetry, another is to write poetry, and the best of all
is to live poetry!" And I remember his saying that at
rare moments he had glimpses of what poetry really
meant, how it solved all problems of conduct and
settled all questions of values. Moreover, it kept

men young, he thought. One night we were sitting at a high window overlooking King's Parade. We had been discussing some philosophical point about the nature of Beauty, when we saw and heard some drunken members of another college going home. "Those fellows," he said, "would think us very old if they had been in this room to-night, but when they go down and sit on office stools, *they* will grow old quite suddenly, and many years hence *we* shall still be talking and thinking about these sorts of things, and we shall still be young."

'As for philosophy, he shared the general view of the set in which we moved that ethics were exceedingly important, but metaphysics rather trivial; that it mattered immensely what was good, but comparatively little what was real. I remember several fierce arguments[1] as to whether a man's character, as distinct from the series of states of mind through which he passed, could be good in itself, and also a controversy as to whether states of affairs, as distinct from the states of mind of the persons concerned in them, could be good in themselves. Rupert maintained that Variety was good in itself. "A world containing you and me and Maynard Keynes," he said, "is obviously better than a world containing three people exactly like any one of us!"'

One of the most significant and absorbing of his activities was the dramatic. Here I must quote from E. J. Dent's admirable record: "When I came back to

[1] *Argument*, it will be remembered, at *The Funeral of Youth*, was 'too full of woe to speak.'

45

Cambridge in the autumn of 1907, I soon became aware that a new spirit was making itself felt. Probably it was active in more ways than I was able to observe; but the first notable result of it was the performance of Marlowe's *Faustus* in November by a number of men who afterwards constituted themselves as the Marlowe Dramatic Society. The new spirit seemed to come partly from Rugby, partly from Bedales, and by an odd coincidence the two leaders, though not related, bore the same name: Rupert and Justin Brooke. It was a queer performance. The elder generation were scandalised almost before the play began: no scenery, only dingy green hangings, no music, no footlights, frequent "black-outs," no names of the actors printed. And all this in the A.D.C. Theatre, with its familiar portraits, its familiar memories! No wonder they were upset by it all. "*Faustus* isn't a play at all"—"absurd for undergraduates to attempt tragedy"—"why didn't they get somebody with experience to coach them?"—"why do they act in the dark?"—"not always in very nice taste." It was indeed a queer performance. Faustus looked absurdly young; Mephistophilis (Rupert), his face completely hidden by his cowl, generally turned his back to the audience, and spoke in a thick indistinct voice which often served merely as a background to the piercing whispers of the Master of ——, whose thirst for information was insatiable. But in spite of these things and many others, in spite of the tedious humour of the comic scenes, the play had a new spirit of its own. The tragic moments were genuinely

46

moving. Crude, awkward, and amateurish as it all
was, there was the spirit of true poetry about it. One
felt that to these actors poetry was the greatest thing
in life.

'The Marlowe group were inclined to be suspicious,
perhaps not unjustly, of anyone who was a member
of the Senate. But as I had been one of the few to
admit themselves sincerely impressed by *Faustus*, I
was occasionally allowed to hear news of their next
project. Milton was to be commemorated in the summer,[1] and the young poets were going to have a hand
in it. Rupert was to be seen almost daily, I believe, in
Room Theta, studying vast books on theatre-con-
struction; a kind friend brought out for him his copy
of the Trinity Milton facsimile, for the settling of
points of textual criticism; and mysterious designs for
costumes and scenery were handed round, in which
wonderful effects *à la* Gordon Craig were to be ob-
tained with scaffold poles.

'It is difficult to criticise *Comus*, or to write the history of its preparation. It had much the same faults
and the same merits as *Faustus*, though on a larger
scale. Rupert was not a good actor,[2] nor even a good
speaker of verse. Yet I feel now that anyone who
remembers *Comus*, and remembers it with ever so

[1] By this time the Authorities had come round to the Marlowe Society, and Christ's College bespoke a special performance of its *Comus* for their celebration of the Tercentenary.

[2] He took the part of the Attendant Spirit. It is only fair to
say that this view of his acting, or at any rate of his elocution,
was far from universal.

slight a sense of beauty, will think of Rupert as the central figure of it; and watching rehearsals daily, as I did, I felt that, however much his personal beauty might count for, it was his passionate devotion to the spirit of poetry that really gave *Comus* its peculiar and indescribable atmosphere.

'*Comus*, however unimportant to the world at large, did, in fact, mean a great deal for Rupert and his friends. It was the first time that he had had to bear the responsibility of a large undertaking, and he addressed himself to it in the spirit of a scholar. It deepened his sense of poetry, of drama, and of music; it made him develop an ideal continually present in his mind, even in later years, which gave solidity to his group, the ideal of Cambridge, of young Cambridge, as the source from which the most vital movements in literature, art, and drama were to spring. *Comus* effected an intimate collaboration of all sorts of brains, and it effected especially a co-operation of men and women. Rupert was by no means the only remarkable person in the circle. He had, moreover, a power of making friends with women as well as with men, and although *Comus* was probably a symptom rather than a cause, it was from about that time that joint societies, such as the Heretics and the Fabians, began to make a new influence felt.'

Rupert was knocked up by his exertions over *Comus*. He wrote from Rugby to Mrs Cornford (then Miss Frances Darwin): 'I went off without even saying good-bye or thank-you to people. My mother (I can plead) packed me up and snatched me here to

48

sleep and recover. I am now convalescent, and can sit up and take a little warm milk-and-Tennyson. I feel a deserter; but I can always adduce the week when the Committee went to the seaside, and I faced the world and Albert's Artistic Temperament alone.'[1]

He had written to his mother about this week, and about another matter. 'Albert [Rutherston], who is painting our scenery, is staying with me. We paint in the theatre, 9 to 5 every day. I daub a little, but most of the time carry and empty pails, run errands, wind pulleys, etc. . . . . . . I suppose you heard of the dreadful tragedy that happened last Saturday week—[Walter] Headlam's death? It was terribly sudden. He was about in King's all the week—kept the procession for the Chancellor's installation on Wednesday waiting for half an hour by being late—in his usual way! On Friday he was in King's, about, as usual. Friday evening he went up to town, had a slight operation (by some accounts), and died on Saturday morning. . . . . . . It made me quite miserable and ill for some days. One gets so *angry* at that sort of thing. I didn't know him *very* well. But he was the one classic I really admired and liked;[2] and I had done a good deal of work with him. The papers made very little of it. He published so little that outside people didn't know much of him. But his friends, and we

[1] It was at about this time that he bought two drawings by Augustus John, 'very splendid ones—even the critical Albert admitted that, and confessed jealousy.'

[2] It was not till later that he knew A. W. Verrall, whom he 'admired and liked' very much.

who were his pupils, knew his great genius. I don't know how much of him they will be able to rake together from his papers. But all the great, ripe, splendid works we all proudly looked forward to him achieving—which we knew he might consummate any time he gave himself a few months, have died with him: can never be made. That's the terrible thing. Even in Cambridge many people knew of him most as a brilliant "scholar," *i.e.*, emender of Greek texts. But he was also about the best writer of Greek there has been since the Greeks. And what I loved so in him was his extraordinary and living appreciation of all English poetry, modern and ancient. To hear him repeat it was a delight. He was an excellent poet himself, and had perfect taste. He first inspired me with a desire to get *Comus* done, a term or two ago, and has often talked about it since. I had made up, in my mind, a little list of things about which I was going to ask him, large and small points, to make certain that we should interpret and understand it in the best way possible; but I put it off till too late. . . . The whole thing makes me so rebellious—to think what the world has lost.'

*   *   *

The vacations were spent in all sorts of ways: at the Fabian Summer School, or camping out with smaller groups of friends; on walking tours; or, at Christmas, with large heterogeneous parties for winter-sports in Switzerland. He told his mother of his plans for one of the Swiss excursions in the winter of 1908. 'What

I meant about the holidays is this. It is quite true that
I have plenty of opportunities of resting. But I always
feel that I oughtn't to, and can't, do nothing. There
are so many things I must learn and do, and there is
not too much time. My brain *must* be working. And
so the only way (I find) I have a real holiday from my
work is on a walking-tour, or in Switzerland; times
and places where it is impossible to think or read for
more than five minutes. In a way such things are a
waste of time. And I can't imagine anything I should
hate more than a long "holiday" like that, of more
than a week or ten days. It would be intolerable.
But, I think, just a week's mental rest strengthens
a mind for some time. This sounds rather priggish;
but I'm really very much in earnest about reading
and writing.'

The Swiss relaxations used to include the performance of a play, or even an opera—*The Importance of
Being Earnest*, in which Rupert played Algernon, or
a nonsense-melodrama written in collaboration by
the party, but mostly by him. In the opera he was
obliged at the last moment, by the sudden defection
of the tenor, to play the hero. He couldn't sing a note;
and the difficulty was got over by making the actor
who played his valet stand beside him in a rigid position and sing, while Rupert did the gestures.

The English holidays were more peaceful. 'Over-
cote is a lovely place,' he wrote to his mother on one
of them, 'with nothing but an old inn, and a ferry.
There are villages round, a mile or two away, but
hidden. And there's just the Ouse, a slow stream, and

some trees and fields, and an immense expanse of sky. There were a lot of wild birds about, wild duck, and snipe, and herons.'

All these occasions produced floods of doggerel, some of which is amusing—from a snatch of blank verse on an unfortunate town-bred friend who arrived late on a wet night at a camp where all the beds were occupied, and didn't rise to the occasion:

> *In the late evening he was out of place,*
> *And infinitely irrelevant at dawn,*

—to the following elaborate ballade, composed during a sleepless night when he and Dudley Ward,[1] coming very late into Cranborne, couldn't find the inn which they had picked out in the guide-book for the sake of its name:

> *In Cranborne town two inns there are,*
>   *And one the Fleur-de-Lys is hight,*
> *And one, the inn Victoria,*[2]
>   *Where, for it was alone in sight,*
>   *We turned in tired and tearful plight*
> *Seeking for warmth, and company,*
>   *And food, and beds so soft and white—*
> *These things are at the Fleur-de-Lys.*
>
> *Where is the ointment for the scar?*
>   *Slippers? and table deftly dight?*

[1] The economist, not to be confused with the Member of Parliament of the same name.

[2] Showing that a Grantchester man can make cockney rhymes just like a Barton man.

Sofas? tobacco? soap? and ah!
  Hot water for a weary wight?
  Where is the food, in toil's despite?
The golden eggs? the toast? the tea?
  The maid so pretty and polite?
These things are at the Fleur-de-Lys.

Oh, we have wandered far and far
  We are fordone and wearied quite.
No lamp is lit; there is no star.
  Only we know that in the night
  We somewhere missed the faces bright,
The lips and eyes we longed to see;
  And Love, and Laughter, and Delight.
These things are at the Fleur-de-Lys.

Prince, it is dark to left and right.
  Waits there an inn for you and me?
Fine noppy ale and red firelight?
  These things are at the Fleur-de-Lys.

The next was written at a very favourite inn, the *Pink and Lily*, near Princes Risborough, on one occasion when he went there with Jacques Raverat.

  Never came there to the Pink
  Two such men as we, I think.
  Never came there to the Lily
  Two men quite so richly silly;[1]

[1] This couplet, which is inconsistent with the rest, was supplied by his companion.

So broad, so supple, and so tall,
So modest and so brave withal,
With hearts so clear, such noble eyes,
Filled with such sage philosophies,
Thirsty for Good, secure of Truth,
Fired by a purer flame than youth,
Serene as age, but not so dirty,
Old, young, mature, being under thirty.
Were ever two so fierce and strong,
Who drank so deep, and laughed so long,
So proudly meek, so humbly proud,
Who walked so far, and sang so loud?

The last I will quote was pinned to some food which
they left by the roadside after luncheon:

Two men left this bread and cake
For whomsoever finds to take.
He and they will soon be dead.
Pray for them that left this bread.

*   *   *

From this time the story shall be told as far as possible in extracts from Rupert Brooke's letters to his
friends, from which his character will appear far more
vividly, and on the whole more clearly, than from
anything that could be written about it. But the picture thus given must for various reasons be incomplete, and perhaps misleading; and a few touches must
here be added, to be borne in mind while the letters
are read.

They might, for instance, give the idea of self-absorption. Self-conscious he was, self-examining, and self-critical, to the last degree; but hardly ever self-absorbed. The extracts cannot show his continual helpfulness and serviceableness to his friends, both in large matters which are too private, and in details which are too trivial, to be chronicled. 'There was a deep-seated generosity in him,' says Mrs Cornford, 'at once sensible and tender. I used to think that the real reason the charm of his face struck people so greatly was because its clearness and fairness were not simply a happy accident of youth, but expressed this innate quality in him. . . . . . He was endlessly kind in helping me with my verses (except that kindness seems the wrong word, because he did it as a matter of course). He would sit for an hour or two at a time, generally on the ground, frowning and biting the end of his pencil and scribbling little notes on the margin before we talked. Of the better things he would only say "I like that," or "That's good." I can't imagine him using a word of that emotional jargon in which people usually talk or write of poetry. He made it feel more like carpentering.' Here we see him as he often was, just simple and serious, full of the business of the moment. Indeed he was very restful to be with. The eager, working, excited brain which shows in the letters, incessantly registering, assimilating, juggling with, sensations and impressions, hid its thrills under an appearance almost of placidity. He never 'put himself forward,' and seldom took the lead, in conversation; Mrs Asquith spoke of 'the beauty of his eyes looking steadily and without mocking into quite ordinary talk.' But he was 'noticing' all the time; he had the power which women are supposed to have of knowing everything that is going on in the room; and he seemed never to forget the smallest detail.

His observation was always, if not 'mocking,' at any rate amused; and something must be said about the peculiar quality of his irony and his humour, which were very intimate, and might be misunderstood by strangers. J. T. Sheppard has written admirably about them, as they played on his friends. 'He would laugh at them, and sometimes treat their most cherished enthusiasms as amusing, if harmless foibles; but he had not the power, possessed by some people who matter less, of making you seem small and dull. His society was, in the good sense, comfortable. He loved children, and when he treated his grown-up friends as rather absurd but very nice children, they would have had to be very absurd indeed to resent it. It must have been very hard to be pompous or priggish in his company.' He treated himself in much the same way. If there was any fun to be got out of a laugh against him, far from grudging it, he gave every facility; but he liked to have the first go at it himself. There was always some foundation for the jokes; but the truth and the fun were inextricably mixed up, and one had to know exactly how many grains of salt to take. As an obvious instance: it was certainly his usual belief that he was, or at any rate had it in him to be, a good poet; and so he would describe himself as the first poet of the age, because it *would* be funny if he thought so, and therefore it was amusing to say so; and there was no risk of his correspondents thinking him cocksure. In the same way he would pick out his best lines for special praise. 'There's one *superb* line,' he said to me when he first showed me the sonnet *Love.* ' "Astonishment is no more in hand or shoulder." Isn't it amazing?' He did think it good, and was enjoying what Keats calls 'the re-perception and ratification of what is fine' in his own work; but he said it with a twinkle.

He always loved to dramatise a situation, and to make out that he had said or done something absurdly striking and stunning. Here is a good illustration from a letter of 1909: 'And so I walked and laughed and met a many people and made a thousand songs—all very good—and, in the end of the days, came to a woman who was more glorious than the sun, and stronger and stranger than the sea, and kinder than the earth, who is a flower made out of fire, a star that laughs all day, whose brain is clean and clear like a man's, and her heart is full of courage and kindness; and whom I love. I told her that the Earth was crowned with windflowers, and dancing down the violet ways of Spring; that Christ had died and Pan was risen; that her mouth was like the sunlight on a gull's wings. As a matter of fact I believe I said "Hullo! isn't it rippin' weather?" '

'You are the only person, Frances,' he wrote much later to Mrs Cornford, 'who ever believed *all* my lies. Nothing (short, perhaps, of incredulity) can shake my devotion to you.'

One more quotation from Sheppard: 'He was kind and unaffected. But he was not miraculously unselfish, nor indifferent to his popularity. The fact that in small things he sometimes seemed to choose the pleasant second-best, and, as he himself realised, rather eagerly to accept the little successes which he could so easily win, should make us appreciate not less, but more, the rightness and the goodness of his larger choices. He was very sensitive to praise, and it would be wrong to say that he was always wisely praised. But he was sensible enough and strong enough to take flattery, in the long run, for what it was worth; and he valued the affection that was critical, not flattering.

'Because he was human, he enjoyed his popularity. The quality which won it was, I think, his power of liking people, and making them feel, because he liked them all, not only at their ease with him, but also happy and friendly with one another. His company had this effect at home, and in his rooms at King's, in his garden at Grantchester, in London, and I am sure wherever he went in Germany and in America. Certainly the most varied people used to delight in it, and he, for his part, was delighted when some of the incongruous persons he liked, unexpectedly also liked one another.

'He was in some ways like a child, very frank and simple, generally knowing what he wanted, and, if he could see it, taking it; but also, where his affections were concerned, most loyal and devoted; suffering acutely in the few great troubles that came to him, but generally confident and happy; above all delighting, and making other people share his delight, in a great number of different things.'

III

He took the Classical Tripos in the summer of 1909, only getting a Second. This was a 'disappointment,' though not specially so to him. 'He found English literature, now, for him, more important than the ancient classics; and he has convinced us all that he was right,' says Sheppard, himself a Don at King's; so there is no need for head-shaking.

After term, he went to live within easy distance of Cambridge, at a house in Grantchester called the Orchard. Here he spent most of the rest of this year, going for the summer holidays to a vicarage his parents had taken at Clevedon in Somerset, which he was allowed to cram with relays of his friends. He was working all these months for the Charles Oldham Shakespeare Prize, which he won in the course of the Michaelmas Term.

He went for Christmas to Switzerland, where he got poisoned by drinking some bad water; and he came home to find his father seriously ill with haemorrhage on the brain. He had to give up Grantchester and Cambridge and all his plans for next term, and undertake the temporary management of the House at Rugby. He wrote to Mrs Cornford to apologise for backing out of his part in *The Land of Heart's Desire.* 'There are other things I'm very sick to miss,' he went on: 'the Marlowe play, and Verrall's lectures, etc.— seeing you all—the whole life of it, in fact. Also I fear I may have confused the Fabians rather by not coming up. I'm a general nuisance. Oh! and I'm so sad and fierce and miserable not to be in my garden and little house at Grantchester all this term. I love being there so much—more than any place I've ever lived in. I love the place and especially the solitude so much. I'd thought of being there when the spring was coming, every day this winter, and dreamt of seeing all the little brown and green things. It's horrible of me to talk like this when I'm in the house with two other people who are infinitely worse off in happiness than I am, and one of them in pain....... Many thanks for your letter, by the way. It cheered me greatly at the exact time when I was sitting gloomily waiting for my father's return from the London doctor, and wondering what the verdict would be. I had sunk into that abysmal darkness which comes on a convalescent when anything goes wrong. I've shaken off my dreadful disease now. It inspired me with thousands of Hardyesque short poems about people whose affairs went dismally wrong, or frightfully detestable people I couldn't help falling in love with, or interviews with the Almighty in which He turned out to be an absolute and unimaginative idiot. . . . But I hope to occupy my exile by composing some work of immortal genius.'

A little later Mr Brooke died suddenly, and was buried on the very day when the fifty boys were coming back to School Field. The shock was great. Rupert wrote to me in March, thanking me for a letter, 'and indeed for the earlier ones to an invalid—though those seem so long ago that I cannot find continuity between that time and this. It is the smallest part of the

gulf that I have been ill again—I collapsed, unforgiv-
ably [with influenza], just after the funeral; and again
subsisted for days on milk and the pieces I could sur-
reptitiously bite out of the end of my thermometer.
Now, and lately, though, I am well and bursting with
activity. I work like a Professor, and feel the Spring in
my bones. I am acting Housemaster in my father's place
till the end of the term. Then we are to be turned from
this place by cold strangers, into a little house with a
patch of grass in front, on a road, stiff and ugly. . . . I
find I am an admirable schoolmaster. I have a bluff
Christian tone that is wholly pedagogic. Also, they
remember I used to play for the School at various violent games, and respect me accordingly.'

'My heart is warm,' he wrote to Jacques Raverat,
'and has been half secure—or confident, rather—
throughout the last four centuries (just a month) because of the splendid people I know. Half are scattered
abroad now. But you'll all meet in April. I'll find all
of you by August.'

Some of them he met himself in April, when he
wrote to me from Lulworth: 'At length I am escaped
from the world's great snare. This is heaven. Downs,
Hens, Cottages, and the Sun. . . . For the rest of Eternity my stabile address is 24 Bilton Road, Rugby.
School Field, that palatial building, will know us no
more. And henceforth I shall have to play on other
people's tennis lawns. I wept copiously last week on
saying good-bye to the three and fifty little boys
whose Faith and Morals I had upheld for ten weeks.
I found I had fallen in love with them all. They were

so pleasant and fresh-minded as they were. And it
filled me with purpureal gloom to know that their
plastic souls would harden into the required shapes,
and they would go to swell the indistinguishable
masses who fill Trinity Hall, Clare, Caius ... and at
last become members of the English Upper, or
Upper Middle, Classes. I am glad I am not going to
be a schoolmaster for ever. The tragedy would be
too great.'

He went back to Grantchester for most of the May
term, and immediately got caught up again in the
multiplicity of Cambridge life. 'I'm afraid there isn't
the ghost of a chance,' he wrote in answer to a sug-
gestion that we should go abroad together for a fortnight. 'I'm so extraordinarily inextricable and necessary! You think this conceit; but it's not. Various
bodies and societies have arranged things in which I
am continuously and hopelessly involved. Also my
labours at the University Library press most insis-
tently upon me. I wish I could have come, it would
have been lovely. Grantchester's lovely though, too.
When are you coming? The apple-blossom and the
river and the sunsets have combined to make me re-
lapse into a more than Wordsworthian communion
with nature, which prevents me reading more than
100 lines a day, or thinking at all.'

His work at this time was on the Elizabethan drama,
mainly for a monograph on 'Puritanism as represented or referred to in the early English drama up to
1642,' with which he won the Harness Prize this year.[1]

[1] A copy of this essay is in the British Museum.

It shows deep reading. 'I read 20 pre-Elizabethan plays a week, all poor,' he had written in March; and in April from Lulworth, 'All the morning I souse myself in Elizabethan plays; and every afternnon I walk up perpendicular places alone for hours'—adding in a moment of surfeit, 'There are no good plays between 1500 and 1650, except the *Faithful Shepherdess*—and, perhaps, *Antony and Cleopatra*.'

By this time he had already written a good many of the poems which were to appear in the 1908–1911 section of his first book, and he was writing more. 'I am slowly recovering from Work,' he wrote to Mrs Cornford. 'Henceforth I am going to lead what Dudley calls "a Life Dedicated to Art." Hurray!' Mrs Cornford and he both had plans for publishing a volume of poems in 1910—(hers was carried out, his postponed). 'They will review us together!' he told her. 'The *Daily Chronicle*, or some such, that reviews verse in lumps, will notice thirty-four minor poets in one day, ending with *Thoughts in Verse on many Occasions, by a Person of Great Sensibility*, by F. Cornford, and *Dead Pansy-Leaves, and other Flowerets*, by R. Brooke; and it will say, "Mr Cornford has some pretty thoughts; but Miss Brooke is always intolerable" (they always guess the sex wrong). And then I shall refuse to call on you. Or another paper will say, " Major Cornford and the Widow Brooke are both bad; but Major Cornford is the worst." And then you will cut me in the street.'

The Marlowe Society's second performance of *Dr*

Faustus, got up for a party of fifty German students who visited Cambridge in August, was one excitement of this summer; and another was a tour with Dudley Ward in a disreputable-looking caravan, to popularise the Minority Report on the Poor Law in the principal towns on the South Coast—except Bournemouth, through which they drove, bareheaded and barefoot, at full speed, in fear or hope of being seen by a Conservative aunt who lived there.

Next month he wrote to F. H. Keeling[1] from Rugby. The letter is dated September 20th–23rd, 1910: 'I've several times started to write you a notable and rhetorical letter, but my life has been too jerky to admit of much connected thought lately, so the letter always fizzled away, and was not. I'm sorry I didn't write sooner, but I wanted to be able to write down a great attack on your pessimism in abundant and reasoned language. And such a thing takes time and thought. Also, I may agree with you.

'What is pessimism? Why do you say you are becoming a pessimist? What does it mean? He may (I say to myself) mean that he thinks that the Universe is bad as a whole, or that it's bad just now, or that, more locally and importantly, things aren't going to get any better in our time and our country, no matter how much we preach Socialism and clean hearts at them.

'Is it the last two? Are you telling us that the world

[1] F. H. Keeling, or as he was always called by his friends, 'Ben' Keeling, the chief figure among the Cambridge Fabians of Rupert's day, was killed in the Somme battle of 1916.

is, after all, bad, and, what's more horrible, without enough seeds of good in it? I, writing poetry and reading books and living at Grantchester all day, feel rather doubtful and ignorant about "the world"— about England, and men, and what they're like. Still, I see some, besides the University gang. I see all these queer provincials in this town, upper and middle and lower class, and God knows they're sterile enough.

'But I feel a placid and healthy physician about it all (only I don't know what drugs to recommend). This is because I've such an overflowing (if intermittent) flood of anti-pessimism in me. I'm using the word now in what I expect is its most important sense, of a feeling rather than a reasoned belief. The horror is not in *believing* the Universe is bad—or even believing the world won't improve—on a reasoned and cool examination of all facts, tendencies and values, so much as in a sort of general *feeling* that there isn't much potentiality for good in the world, and that anyhow it's a fairly dreary business—an absence of much appreciation and hope, and a somehow paralysed will for good. As this is a feeling, it *may* be caused by reason and experience, or more often by loneliness or soul-measles or indigestion or age or anything else. And it can equally be cured by other things than reason—by energy or weather or good people, as well as by a wider ethical grasp. At least, so I've found in the rather slight and temporary fits of depression I've had, in exile or otherwise, lately—or even in an enormous period of Youthful Tragedy with which I started at Cambridge. I have a remedy. It is a dangerous one, but I think very good on the whole; though it may lead to a sterile but ecstatic content, or even to the asylum. In practice, I find, it doesn't—or hasn't yet—make me inefficient. (I am addressing an Adult School on Sunday. I have started a group for studying the Minority Report here. I am going to Cambridge in a week to oversee, with the light of pure reason, the powerful energies of those who are setting forth the new Fabian Rooms,—and later, to put the rising generation, Fabian and otherwise, on the way of Light, all next term.)

'The remedy is Mysticism, or Life, I'm not sure which. Do not leap or turn pale at the word Mysticism, I do not mean any religious thing, or any form of belief. I still burn and torture Christians daily. It is merely the *feeling*—or a kindred one—which underlay the mysticism of the wicked mystics, only I refuse to be cheated by the *feeling* into any kind of *belief*. They were convinced by it that the world was very good, or that the Universe was one, or that God existed. I don't any the more believe the world to be good. Only I do get rid of the despair that it isn't—and I certainly seem to see additional possibilities of its getting better.

'It consists in just looking at people and things as themselves—neither as useful nor moral nor ugly nor anything else; but just as being. At least, that's a philosophical description of it. What happens is that I suddenly feel the extraordinary value and importance of everybody I meet, and almost everything I see. In *things* I am moved in this way especially by some things: but in people by almost all people. That is, when the mood is on me. I roam about places—yesterday I did it even in Birmingham!—and sit in trains and see the essential glory and beauty of all the people I meet. I can watch a dirty middle-aged trades-man in a railway-carriage for hours, and love every dirty greasy sulky wrinkle in his weak chin and every button on his spotted unclean waistcoat. I know their states of mind are bad. But I'm so much occupied with their being there at all, that I don't have time to think of that. I tell you that a Birmingham gouty Tariff Reform fifth-rate business man is splendid and immortal and desirable.

'It's the same about the things of ordinary life. Half an hour's roaming about a street or village or railway-station shows so much beauty that it's impossible to be anything but wild with suppressed exhilaration. And it's not only beauty and beautiful things. In a flicker of sunlight on a blank wall, or a reach of muddy pave-ment, or smoke from an engine at night, there's a sudden significance and importance and inspiration that makes the breath stop with a gulp of certainty and happiness. It's not that the wall or the smoke seem important for anything, or suddenly reveal any general statement, or are rationally seen to be good or beautiful in themselves,—only that *for you* they're per-fect and unique. It's like being in love with a person. One doesn't (nowadays, and if one's clean-minded) think the person better or more beautiful or larger than the truth. Only one is extraordinarily excited that the person, exactly as he is, uniquely and splen-

didly just exists. It's a feeling, not a belief. Only it's a
feeling that has amazing results. I suppose my occupa-
tion is being in love with the universe—or (for it's
an important difference) with certain spots and
moments and points of it.

'I wish to God I could express myself. I have a vague
notion that this is all very incoherent. But the upshot
of it is that one's too happy to *feel* pessimistic; and too
much impressed by the immense value and potenti-
alities of everything to *believe* in pessimism—for the
following reason, and in the following sense. Every
action, one knows (as a good Determinist), has an
eternal effect. And every action, therefore, which
leads on the whole to good, is *"frightfully"* important.
For the good mystic knows how jolly "good" is. It is
not a question of either getting to Utopia in the year
2000, or not. There'll be so much good then, and so
much evil. And we can affect it. There—from the
purely rational point of view—is the beginning and
end of the whole matter. It oughtn't to make any
difference to our efforts whether the good in 2000 A.D.
will be a lot greater than it is now, or a little greater,
or less. In any case, the amount of good we can cause
by doing something, or can subtract by not doing it,
remains about the same. And that is all that ought
to matter.

'Lately, when I've been reading up the Elizabethans,
and one or two other periods, I've been amazed more
than ever at the way things change. Even in talking to
my uncle of seventy about the Victorians, it comes out
astoundingly. The whole machinery of life, and the

minds of every class and kind of man, change beyond recognition every generation. I don't know that "Progress" is certain. All I know is that change is. These solid solemn provincials, and old maids, and business men, and all the immovable system of things I see round me, will vanish like smoke. All this present overwhelming reality will be as dead and odd and fantastic as crinolines, or "a dish of tay." Something will be in its place, inevitably. And what that something will be, depends on me. With such superb work to do, and with the wild adventure of it all, and with the other minutes (too many of them) given to the enchantment of being even for a moment alive in a world of real matter (not that imitation, gilt stuff one gets in Heaven) and actual people,—I have no time now to be a pessimist.

'I don't know why I have scribbled down these thin insane vapourings. I don't suppose you're still as desperate as you were when you wrote in June. When are you coming to Cambridge? I am going to Germany for the spring term. But if you can get there next term, are you coming out to stay at Grantchester? I lead a lovely and dim and rustic life there, and have divine food. Hugh is going to be in London, and —— is old as the hills and withered as a spider, and I am the oldest Fabian left (except ——, who is senile), and I dodder about and smile with toothless gums on all the gay young sparks of the Fabian Society, to whom I am more than a father.

'So you might tell me if you are going to shake off for a day or a month the ghastly coils of British

Family Life and of Modern Industry that you are wound in, and come to see the bovine existence of a farmer.

'In the name of God and the Republic,

RUPERT.'

The next event was a journey on the Continent at the beginning of 1911. He conceived romantic plans for it, as appears in the latter part of this letter to Geoffrey Fry, written before he started, to thank for a present of Mr Bullen's Elizabethan Songbooks: 'I read them when I ought to be learning German, and I writhe with vain passion and with envy. How did they do it? Was it, as we're told, because they always wrote to tunes? The lightness! There are moments when I try to write "songs," "where Lumpkin with his Giles hob-nobs," but they are bumping rustic guffaws. I feel that sense of envious incompetence and a vast angry clumsiness that hippopotamuses at the Zoo must feel when you stand before them with your clouded cane and take snuff. They're occasionally—the songbooks, not the hippopotamuses—so like the Anthology, and oh! I can see why Headlam loved them.

'I may see you yet in England. For I don't go till January 8 or so. But when I do go, aha! England will never see me more. I shall grow my red whiskers and take to Art. In a few years you may come and stay with me in my villa at Sybaris, or my palace near Smyrna, or my tent at Kandahar, or my yacht off the Cyclades. But you will be a respectable lawyer. You will waggle your pince-nez and lecture me on my

70

harem. Then a large one-eyed negro Eunuch will
come and tie you up and pitch you into the sea. And
I shall continue to paint sea-scapes in scarlet and
umber.'

These dreams were not realised. He began his travels
with three months in Munich, where he wrote to
Mrs. Cornford in the middle of February: 'The worst
of solitude—or the best—is, that one begins poking
at his own soul, examining it, cutting the soft and rotten parts away. And where's one to stop? Have you
ever had, at lunch or dinner, an over-ripe pear or
apple, and, determined to make the best of it, gone on
slicing off the squashy bits? You may imagine me, in
München, at a German lunch with Life, discussing
hard, and cutting away at the bad parts of the desert.
"Oh!" says Life, courteous as ever, "I'm sure you've
got a bad soul there. Please don't go on with it!
Leave it, and take another! I'm so sorry!" But, knowing I've taken the last, and polite anyhow, "Oh, no,
please!" I say, scraping away. "It's really all right. It's
only a little gone, here and there, on the outside.
There's plenty that's quite good. I'm quite enjoying
it. You always have such delightful souls!". . . And
after a minute, when there's a circle of messy brown
rounding my plate, and in the centre a rather woe-
begone brown-white thin shapeless scrap, the centre
of the thing, Life breaks in again, seeing my plight.—
"Oh, but you can't touch any of that! It's bad right
through! I'm sure Something must have got into it!
Let me ring for another! There's sure to be some in the
larder.". . . But it won't do, you know. So I rather

ruefully reply, "Ye-es, I'm afraid it *is* impossible. But I won't have another, thanks. I don't really want one at all. I only took it out of mere greed, and to have something to do. Thank you, I've had quite enough —such excellent meat and pudding! I've done splendidly—BUT TO GO ON WITH OUR CONVERSATION ABOUT LITERATURE,—YOU WERE SAYING, I THINK . . .?" and so the incident's at an end.

'Dear! dear! it's very trying being so exalted one day and ever so desperate the next—this Self-knowledge (*why* did that old fool class it with Self-reverence and Self-control? They're rarely seen together!) But so one lives in Munich.

'—And then your letter came! So many thanks. It made me shake with joy to know that Cambridge and England (as I know it) was all as fine as ever. That Jacques and Ka should be sitting in a café, looking just like themselves—oh God! what an incredibly lovely superb world. I fairly howled my triumph down the ways of this splendid city. "Oh! you fat, muddy-faced, grey, jolly Germans who despise me because I don't know your rotten language! Oh! the people I know, and you don't! Oh! you poor things!" And they all growl at me because they don't know why I glory over them. But of course, part of the splendour is that—if they only knew it—they too, these Germans, are all sitting in cafés and looking just like themselves. That knowledge sets me often dreaming in a vague, clerical, world-misty spirit over my solitary coffee, in one of the innumerable cafés here in which I spend my days. I find myself smiling a dim, gentle, poetic, paternal, Jehovah-like smile over the ultimate excellence of humanity—at people of, obviously, the most frightful lives and reputations at other tables; who come presently sidling towards me. My mysticism vanishes, and in immense terror I fly suddenly into the street.

'Oh, but they're a kindly people. Every night I sit in a café near here, after the opera, and read the day-old *Times* (!) and drink—prepare to hear the depths of debauchery into which the young are led in these wicked foreign cities!—HOT MILK, a large glassful. Last night I spilt the whole of the hot milk over myself, while I was trying to negotiate the Literary Supplement. You've no idea how much of one a large glass of hot milk will cover. I was entirely white, except for my scarlet face. All the people in the café crowded round and dabbed me with dirty pocket-handkerchiefs. A kindly people. Nor did I give in. I ordered more hot milk and finished my Supplement, damp but International.

'No! Cambridge isn't very dim and distant, nor Dent a pink shade. I somehow manage, these days, to be aware of two places at once. I used to find it wasn't worth while; and to think that the great thing was to let go completely of a thing when you've done with it, and turn wholly and freshly to the next. "Being able to take and to let go and to take, and knowing when to take and when to let go, and knowing that life's this—is the only way to happiness" is the burden of the Marschallin in the *Rosencavalier* (the rage of Germany just now). There's some truth in it. But

73

sometimes, now, I find I can weave two existences together and enjoy both, and be aware of the unique things of each. It's true that as I write there's an attitude of Jacques's, or a slow laugh of Ka's, or a moon at Grantchester, or a speech of Dickinson's, that I'd love, and that I'm missing. But there'll be other such, no doubt, in May and June—and what if I'd not met the lovable Mr Leuba (and so differently lovable from an English unsuccessful journalist!) or the fascinating Miss Something or Other of Paris, or the interesting and wicked di Ravelli, or Dr Wolfskell who is shy and repeats Swinburne in large quantities with a villainous German accent but otherwise knows no English, or that bearded man in the café, or the great Hegedus, or Professor Sametscu? . . .

'Eh, but I have grown clerical and solemn and moral. That is because I've been seeing so much Ibsen lately. I apologise. I'm old-fashioned enough to admire that man vastly. I've seen five or six of his plays in four weeks. They always leave me prostrate.

'No, I've not yet been proposed to by young ladies in plaid blouses, not even one at a time. As a matter of fact I know only one or two such. Most of the people I see are working at some sensible thing like writing, music, or painting, and are free and comradely. I made one or two incursions into Anglo-German Philistia, and came hurriedly forth. I'm damnably sorry for the plaid blouses (who *do* exist there, and are, at present, so much better than their mothers). I saw two stifling and crying. But I'm not going back to rescue them.

'But in ordinary, and nicer, ways I meet a lot of jolly people. It's true, a lot, I think, what you say about friends; but oh, dear people! it *is* fun going away and making thousands of acquaintances.

'I finish this tourist's effusion at 2 o' the morning, sitting up in bed, with my army blanket round me. My feet, infinitely disconnected, and southward, inform me that to-night it is freezing again. The bed is covered with Elizabethan and German books I may or may not read ere I sleep. In the distance glimmers the gaunt white menacing Ibsenite stove that casts a gloom over my life. The Algerian dancing-master next door is, for once, quiet. I rather think the Dragon overhead (The Dragon = that monstrous, tired-faced, screeching, pouchy creature, of infinite age and horror, who screams opposite me at dinner and talks with great crags of food projecting from her mouth; a decayed Countess, they say) is snoring.

'Oh, I sometimes make a picture of Conduit Head, with Jacques in a corner, and Gwen on other cushions, and Justin on his back, and Ka on a footstool, and Francis smoking, and Frances in the chair to the right (facing the fire). . . . It stands out against the marble of the Luitpold Café and then fades. . . . But say it's true!

'Even with an enormous stomach and a beard and in Munich.—Yours,   RUPERT.'

From Munich he went to join his godfather, Mr Robert Whitelaw, in Florence, where he wrote to me at the end of April: 'I led a most noisome life in Munich, crawling about in trams, and eating, and sleeping. I never thought, and barely ever read. I worked hard in an intermittent doleful way, but never accomplished anything. I spent two months over a poem that describes the feelings of a fish, in the metre of *L'Allegro*. It was meant to be a lyric, but has turned into a work of 76 lines with a moral end. It's quite unintelligible. Beyond that I have written one or two severe and subtle sonnets in my most modern manner —descriptions of very poignant and complicated situations in the life of to-day, thrilling with a false simplicity. The one beginning

" I did not think you thought I knew you knew" has created a sensation in English-speaking circles in Munich.

'I have sampled and sought out German culture. It has changed all my political views. I am widly in favour of nineteen new Dreadnoughts. German culture must never, never prevail! The Germans are nice, and well-meaning, and they try; but they are SOFT. Oh! they *are* soft! The only good things (outside music perhaps) are the writings of Jews who live in Vienna. Have you ever heard of Mr Schnitzler's historical play? They act an abbreviated version which lasts from 7 to 12. I saw it. A Hebrew journalist's version of the *Dynasts*, but rather good.

'Here I live in a *pension* surrounded by English clergymen and ladies. They are all Forster characters. Perhaps it is his *pension*.[1] But to live among Forster

[1] See E. M. Forster's *A Room with a View*.

characters is too bewildering. The "quaint" remarks
fall all round one during mealtimes, with little soft
plups like pats of butter. "So strong," they said, next
to me, at the concert last night, of the Fifth Symphony;
"and yet so restful, my dear! not at all what I should
call *morbid*, you know!" Just now the young parson
and his wife, married a fortnight, have been con-
versing. "Are you ready to kick off?" he said. How
extraordinary! What does it mean? I *gathered* it merely
meant was she dressed for San Lorenzo. But does the
Church talk like that nowadays?

'So I am seeing life. But I am thirsting for Grantchester. I am no longer to be at *The Orchard*, but next
door at *The Old Vicarage*, with a wonderful garden.
I shall fly from Florence, which is full of painstaking
ugly pictures. But before I go I've got to settle the
question, "Shall I lay a handful of roses on Mrs
Browning's grave? and, if so, how many?" These
literary problems are dreadful. And the English Ceme-
tery is so near!'

'It's very late,' he wrote one evening to the Raverats. 'The stars over Fiesole are wonderful; and there
are quiet cypresses and a straight white wall opposite.
I renounce England; though at present I've the senile
affection of a godfather for it. I think of it, over there
(beyond even Fiesole)—Gwen and Jacques and Ka
and Frances and Justin and Dudley, and Dr Verrall
and the Master, and Lord Esher and Mr Balfour.
Good-night, children.'

77

IV

THE Old Vicarage, which was his home in 1911, is a long, low, ramshackle, tumble-down one-storied house, with attics in a high roof, and a verandah. It has a profuse, overgrown, sweet-smelling, 'most individual and bewildering' garden, with random trees and long grass, and here and there odd relics of the eighteenth century, a sundial sticking out from the dried-up basin of a round pond, and an imitation ruin in a corner. Towards the end of the year it is a little melancholy. 'The garden,' he wrote in September, 'is immeasurably autumnal, sad, mysterious, august. I walk in it feeling like a fly crawling on the score of the Fifth Symphony'; and in December he called it a House of Usher. But in summer it's a paradise of scent and colour. 'You'll find me quite wild with reading and the country,' he wrote in an invitation. 'Come prepared for bathing, and clad in primitive clothes. Bring books also: one talks eight hours, reads eight, and sleeps eight.'

Here is a morning of about this time, in a letter to Miss Katherine Cox: 'I worked till 1, and then ran nearly to Haslingfield and back before lunch, thinking over the next bits. There was such clearness and frosty sun. Some men under a haystack, eating their lunch, shouted how fine a day it was. I shouted back it was very cold; and ran on. They roared with laughter and shouted after me that with that fine crop of hair I oughtn't to be cold. . . . It was wonderful and very clean out there. I thought of all you Londoners, dirty

78

old drivellers! Now I'm come in to rehearse my nigger part [as a super in the *Magic Flute*] and to work. I've realised that taking part in theatrical performances is the only thing worth doing. And it's so *very* nice being an intelligent subordinate. I'm a very good subordinate—it's such a test! I'm thought not to dance well: but my intelligence and devotion have brought me rapidly to the front. I am now the most important of 7 negroes!'

He was now working at the first draft of his dissertation on John Webster, which he sent in at the end of the year. 'I've wallowed in Webster-Texts all day,' he wrote in September. 'If only I didn't want, at the same time, to be reading everything else in the world, I should be infinitely happy.' He didn't get the Fellowship till 1913.

He was also preparing the book of *Poems* which Messrs Sidgwick & Jackson published in December. It had a mixed reception, both from his friends and from the critics. I was lucky enough to take it in a way which pleased him; and he rewarded me with the following letter, which is too informing to be left out, though I would rather it fell to someone else to print it: 'Your letter gave me great joy. I horribly feel that degrading ecstasy that I have always despised in parents whose shapeless offspring are praised for beauty. People are queer about my poems. Some that I know very well and have great *sympathie* with, don't like them. Some people seem to like them. Some like only the early ones—them considerably, but the others not at all. These rather sadden me. I hobnob vaguely with them over the promising verses of a young poet, called Rupert Brooke, who died in 1908. But I'm so much more concerned with the living; who doesn't interest them. God! it's so cheering to find someone who likes the modern stuff, and appreciates what one's at. You can't think how your remarks and liking thrilled me. You seemed, both in your classing them and when you got to details, to agree so closely with what I felt about them (only, of course, I often feel doubtful about their relative value to other poetry) that I knew you understood what they meant. It sounds a poor compliment—or else a queer conceitedness—to remark on your understanding them; but it's really been rather a shock to me—and made me momentarily hopeless—that so many intelligent and well-tasted people didn't seem to have any idea what I was driving at, in any poem of the last few years. It opened my eyes to the fact that people who like poetry are barely more common than people who like pictures.

'I'm (of course) unrepentant about the "unpleasant" poems.[1] I don't claim great merit for the *Channel Passage*: but the point of it was (or should have been!) "serious." There are common and sordid things— situations or details—that may suddenly bring all tragedy, or at least the brutality of actual emotions, to you. I rather grasp relievedly at them, after I've beaten vain hands in the rosy mists of poets' experiences. Lear's button, and Hilda Lessways turning the

[1] I had expressed an apologetic preference for poems that I could read at meals.

gas suddenly on, and—but you know more of them
than I. Shakespeare's not unsympathetic—"My mistress' eyes are nothing like the sun." And the emotions
of a sea-sick lover seem to me at least as poignant as
those of the hero who has "brain-fever.". . . . . .

'Mrs Cornford tried to engage me in a controversy
over the book—she and her school. They are known
as the Heart-criers, because they believe all poetry
ought to be short, simple, naïve, and a cry from the
heart; the sort of thing an inspired only child might
utter if it was in the habit of posing to its elders. They
object to my poetry as unreal, affected, complex,
"literary," and full of long words. I'm re-writing English literature on their lines. Do you think this is a fair
rendering of Shakespeare's first twenty sonnets, if
Mrs Cornford had had the doing of them?

TRIOLET

'If you would only have a son,
William, the day would be a glad one.
It would be nice for everyone,
If you would only have a son.
And, William, what would you have done
If Lady Pembroke hadn't had one?
If you would only have a son,
William, the day would be a glad one!

It seems to me to have got the kernel of the situation,
and stripped away all unnecessary verbiage or conscious adornment.'

The verdicts of the newspapers varied from that of

the *Saturday Review*, which 'definitely told Mr Rupert Brooke to "mar no more trees with writing love-songs in their barks,"' to that of the *Daily Chronicle*, which prophesied, by the mouth of Edward Thomas, that he would be a poet, and not a little one. It may be said that in general the book was received with a good deal of interest, and hailed as at least promising. Many of the critics seemed so struck with the 'unpleasant' poems (seven, at most, out of fifty) that they could hardly notice the others. This showed, perhaps, a wrong sense of proportion; but the author's own point of view about them is certainly a matter of interest, and though the purpose of this memoir is not critical, it may be worth while here to put together some of its factors, besides those which appear from the letter I have just quoted. It is, of course, absurdly untrue that, as has been said, he felt he ought to make up for his personal beauty by being ugly in his poetry. To begin with, ugliness had a quite unaffected attraction for him; he thought it just as *interesting* as anything else; he didn't like it—he loathed it—but he liked thinking about it. 'The poetical character,' as Keats said, 'lives in gusto.' Then he still had at this age (twenty-four) a good deal of what soon afterwards faded completely away—the bravado, the feeling that it was fun to shock and astonish the respectable, which came out in his school letters. Again, he was incensed by the usual attitude of criticism—in his view, either stupid or hypocritical—towards 'coarseness' in literature. 'Indeed,' he wrote early this year in a review, 'the Elizabethans *were* unrefined. Their stories were

shocking, their thoughts nasty, their language indeli
cate. It is absurd to want them otherwise. It is intolerable that these critics should shake the pedagogic
finger of amazed reproval at them. . . . . . Such
people do not understand that the vitality of the
Elizabethan Drama is inseparable from [its coarseness].
Their wail that its realism is mingled with indecency
is more than once repeated. True literary realism,
they think, is a fearless reproduction of what real
living men say when there is a clergyman in the
room.' The feeling here expressed urged him to make
a demonstration; it dignified the boyish impulse into
a duty.

To conclude this subject I will quote a letter to his
publisher about the sonnet *Libido*, to which the original title *Lust* is now restored: 'My own feeling is
that to remove it would be to overbalance the book
still more in the direction of unimportant prettiness.
There's plenty of that sort of wash in the other pages
for the readers who like it. They needn't read the
parts which are new and serious. About a lot of the
book I occasionally feel that like Ophelia I've turned
"thought and affliction, passion, hell itself, to favour
and to prettiness." So I'm extra keen about the places
where I think that thought and passion are, however
clumsily, *not* so transmuted. This was one of them. It
seemed to have qualities of reality and novelty that
made up for the clumsiness. . . . I should like it to
stand, as a representative in the book of abortive poetry against literary verse; and because I can't see any
æsthetic ground against it which would not damn

three-quarters of the rest of the book too; or any moral ground at all.'

During all this time he was working up to a rather serious illness. As a child and as a boy he had been delicate, but at Cambridge his health had greatly improved, and all the time he was there he never had to go to a doctor. Now, however, he left his open-air life and came to London for work on Webster. 'He lived,' his Mother tells me, 'in wretched rooms in Charlotte Street, spending all day at the British Museum, going round to his friends in the evening and sitting up most of the night. He then went to Grantchester to finish his dissertation, and from his brother's account scarcely went to bed at all for a week, several times working all night. He came home for Christmas quite tired out.' The letter to me which I last quoted, written at Rugby on the 22nd of December, ends with this: 'I'm sorry I never saw you again. The last part of November and the first of December I spent in writing my dissertation at Grantchester. . . . . . . I couldn't do it at all well. I came to London in a dilapidated condition for a day or two after it was over. Now I'm here over Christmas. About the 27th I go to Lulworth with a reading-party for a fortnight. Then to the South of France, then Germany . . . and the future's mere mist. I want to stay out of England for some time. (1) I don't like it. (2) I want to work —a play, and so on. (3) I'm rather tired and dejected. 'So I *probably* shan't be in London for some time. If I am, I'll let you know. I'm going to try to do scraps

—reviewing, etc.—in my spare time for the immediate future. I suppose you don't edit a magazine? I might review Elizabethan books at some length for the *Admiralty Gazette* or *T.A.T.* (Tattle amongst Tars), or whatever journal you officially produce? At least I hope you'll issue an order to include my poems in the library of all submarines.'

His next letter is of February 25th, 1912, from Rugby: 'I went to Lulworth after Christmas for a reading party. There I collapsed suddenly into a foodless and sleepless Hell. God! how one can suffer from what my amiable specialist described as a "nervous breakdown." (He reported that I had got into a "seriously introspective condition"! and—more tangibly—that my weight had gone down a stone or two.) I tottered, being too tired for suicide, to Cannes, not because I like the b—— place, but because my mother happened to be there. I flapped slowly towards the surface there; and rose a little more at Munich. I have come here for a month or two to complete it. After that I shall be allowed (and, by Phœbus, able, I hope) to do some work. My cure consists in perpetual overeating and over-sleeping, no exercise, and no thought. Rather a nice existence, but oh God! weary.'

In March he went for a walk in Sussex with James Strachey, and sent Miss Cox a sensational account, dated from 'The Mermaid Club, Rye,' of an unsuccessful attempt to visit a great man whose acquaintance he had made at Cambridge. 'I read the "Way of All Flesh" and talk to James. James and I have been out this evening to call on Mr Henry James at 9.0. We found—at length—the house. It was immensely rich, and brilliantly lighted at every window on the ground floor. The upper floors were deserted: one black window open. The house is straight on the street. We nearly fainted with fear of a company. At length I pressed the Bell of the Great Door—there was a smaller door further along, the servants' door we were told. No answer. I pressed again. At length a slow dragging step was heard within. It stopped inside the door. We shuffled. Then, very slowly, very loudly, immense numbers of chains and bolts were drawn within. There was a pause again. Further rattling within. Then the steps seemed to be heard retreating. There was silence. We waited in a wild agonising stupefaction. The house was dead silent. At length there was a shuffling noise from the servants' door. We thought someone was about to emerge from there to greet us. We slid down towards it— nothing happened. We drew back and observed the house. A low whistle came from it. Then nothing for two minutes. Suddenly a shadow passed quickly across the light in the window nearest the door. Again nothing happened. James and I, sick with surmise, stole down the street. We thought we heard another whistle, as we departed. We came back here shaking —we didn't know at what.

'If the evening paper, as you get this, tells of the murder of Mr Henry James—you'll know.'

By this time he was quite well again. He went to Germany in April, and stayed there for two or three months, mostly with Dudley Ward in Berlin, where he wrote *The Old Vicarage, Grantchester*[1] ('this hurried stuff,' he called it when he sent it me). 'I read Elizabethans for 2-3 hours a day, quite happily,' he wrote to his Mother. 'Other work I haven't tried much. I started a short play, and worked at it for two or three hours. I paid the penalty by not getting to sleep till 5 next morning.' The play was a one-act melodrama called *Lithuania*, founded on the well-known anecdote of a son coming back with a fortune, after years of absence in America, to his peasant-family, who kill him for his money and then find out who he was. (It was acted in the spring of 1916 by Miss Lillah M'Carthy, Miss Clare Greet, Leon M. Lion, John Drinkwater, and others, at a charity matinee at His Majesty's, together with Gordon Bottomley's *King Lear's Wife* and Wilfred Gibson's *Hoops*; and was thought to show much promise of dramatic power.)

He came home from Germany as well as ever, to spend the rest of the summer at Grantchester.

I must here touch upon a change in his outlook, a development of his character, which, as I think, took form during this year from the germs which may be seen in his earlier letters, already quoted, to Mr Cotterill and to Ben Keeling. Perhaps it was the result of the 'introspection' which contributed to his illness, and to which his illness in its turn gave opportunity. To put it briefly and bluntly, he had discovered that

[1] This poem was first published in the King's magazine *Basileon*. The MS. is now in the Fitzwilliam Museum.

goodness was the most important thing in life—'that immortal beauty and goodness,' as he wrote much later, 'that radiance, to love which is to feel one has safely hold of eternal things.' Since he grew up he had never held (and did not now acquire) any definite, still less any ready-made, form of religious belief; his ideals had been mainly intellectual; and if he had been asked to define goodness, he would probably have said that it meant having true opinions about ethics. Now he found that it was even more a matter of the heart and of the will; and he did not shrink from avowing his changed view to his old comrades in the life of the mind, some of whom perhaps found it a little disconcerting, a little ridiculous.

Henceforward the only thing that he cared for—or rather felt he ought to care for—in a man, was the possession of goodness; its absence, the one thing that he hated, sometimes with fierceness. He never codified his morals, never made laws for the conduct of others, or for his own; it was the spirit, the passion, that counted with him. 'That is the final rule of life, the best one ever made,' he wrote next year from the Pacific,—' "Whoso shall offend one of these little ones"—remembering that all the eight hundred millions on earth, except oneself, are the little ones.'

In the autumn of this year he began coming to London oftener and for longer visits, usually staying at my rooms in Gray's Inn; going to plays and music halls, seeing pictures, and making numbers of new acquaintances and friends. Henry James, W. B. Yeats

and John Masefield he knew already; and he made
friends about this time with Edmund Gosse, Walter
de la Mare, Wilfrid Gibson, John Drinkwater, W. H.
Davies, and many others.

There was a general feeling among the younger poets
that modern English poetry was very good, and sadly
neglected by readers. Rupert announced one evening,
sitting half-undressed on his bed, that he had conceived a brilliant scheme. He would write a book of
poetry, and publish it as a selection from the works
of twelve different writers, six men and six women,
all with the most convincing pseudonyms. That, he
thought, *must* make them sit up. It occurred to me
that as we both believed there were at least twelve
flesh-and-blood poets whose work, if properly thrust
under the public's nose, had a good chance of pro-
ducing the effect he desired, it would be simpler to
use the material which was ready to hand. Next day
(September 20th it was) we lunched in my rooms
with Gibson and Drinkwater, and Harold Monro and
Arundel del Re (editor and sub-editor of the then
Poetry Review, since re-named *Poetry and Drama*),
and started the plan of the book which was published in December under the name of *Georgian
Poetry*, 1911–1912.

This was our great excitement for the rest of the
year. Rupert went to stay with Ward in Berlin for
November, and kept sending suggestions for pro-
moting the sale of the book. (Years before, a cynical
young friend of ours at King's, Francis Birrell, had
told me that though 'Rupert's public form was the

youthful poet, the real foundation of his character was a hard business faculty.') 'I forget all my other ideas,' he wrote, after making some very practical proposals, 'but they each sold some 25 copies. I have a hazy vision of incredible *réclame*. You ought to have an immense map of England (*vide* "Tono-Bungay") and plan campaigns with its aid. And literary charts, each district mapped out, and a fortress secured. John Buchan to fill a page of the *Spectator*: Filson Young in the *P.M.G.* (we shall be seventeen *Things that Matter* in italics?), etc., etc. You'll be able to found a hostel for poor Georgians on the profits.' Some of his ideas were too vast, but others were acted on; and though delays of printing and binding kept the book back till a few days before Christmas, frustrating our calculation on huge sales to present-givers, its success outran our wildest hopes.

He spent most of the spring of 1913 in London, enjoying himself in many directions. He went again and again to the Russian Ballet, which he loved ('They, if anything can, redeem our civilisation,' he had written in December. 'I'd give everything to be a ballet-designer'); and he conceived a passion for the Hippodrome Revue, *Hullo, Ragtime!* which he saw ten times. He had always been on occasion a great fitter-in of things and people, and vast networks of his minute arrangements survive on postcards, though without the finishing strands put in by telephone. He got to know more and more people, including the Asquith family and George Wyndham, with whom we spent a Sunday at Clouds. He had no ambition for the career of a 'young man about town'; but he felt he might let himself go for the moment, as he would be starting for America before he could get too much involved.

He got his Fellowship on March 8th. 'It's very good of you to congratulate me,' he wrote to Geoffrey Fry. ' You can't think how I despise you mere civilians, now. *Jetzt bin ich Professor.* A grey look of learning has already settled on my face. And I wear spectacles.' Next week he went to King's to be admitted, or, as he called it, 'churched.' 'I dined solemnly,' he told Mrs Cornford, 'with very old white-haired men, at one end of a vast dimly-lit hall, and afterwards drank port somnolently in the Common Room, with the College silver, and 17th Century portraits, and a 16th Century fireplace, and 15th Century ideas. The perfect Don, I...'

The only other break in the London life was a visit to Rugby towards the end of March, when he wrote a rapturous spring-letter to Miss Cathleen Nesbitt. 'But oh! but oh! such a day! "Spring came complete with a leap in a day," said the wisest and nicest man in Warwickshire—my godfather,[1] an aged scholar, infinitely learned in Greek, Latin, English, and Life. He said it was a quotation from Browning. It certainly fitted. I took him a walk. The air had changed all in a night, and had that soft caressingness, and yet made you want to jump and gambol. *Alacer*, and not *acer*, was, we agreed, the epithet for the air. Oh! it's mad to be in London with the world like this. I can't tell you of it. The excitement and music of the birds,

[1] Mr Whitelaw.

the delicious madness of the air, the blue haze in the distance, the straining of the hedges, the green mist of shoots about the trees—oh, it wasn't in these details—it was beyond and round them—something that included them. It's the sort of day that brought back to me what I've had so rarely for the last two years—that tearing hunger to do and do and do things. I want to walk 1000 miles, and write 1000 plays, and sing 1000 poems, and drink 1000 pots of beer, and kiss 1000 girls, and—oh, a million things! . . . . . . The spring makes me almost ill with excitement. I go round corners on the roads shivering and nearly crying with suspense, as one did as a child, fearing some playmate in waiting to jump out and frighten one.'

V

ON May 22nd he started for New York on a year's travels. 'You won't see me again till I'm a bold, bad, bearded broncho-buster in a red shirt and riding breeches,' he wrote to Miss Sybil Pye. His plans were vague, and at that time he expected to be back by the end of 1913. He had written to his mother in February, to explain : 'I think, now my physical health is quite all right, I shall go off to America or somewhere. I feel just as I did in the autumn, that it's no good going on in England. . . . . . . It is only wasting time to go on without doing proper work. I think of going off to California or somewhere, and doing some kind of work, or tramping. I shall take what money I have, and if they don't give me a fellowship, I can capitalise

£200 or so, and that'll last me for as long as I want to be abroad. I have no fear about being able to make a living now, for there are so many papers that'll print anything by me whenever I like.'

'We may meet again in this world,' he wrote to the Raverats, 'I brown and bearded, you mere red round farmers. When that'll be, I know not. Perhaps in six months. Perhaps in six years. Or we may only find each other in a whiter world, nighty-clad, harped, winged, celibate.

> '*Shall we go walks along the hills of Heaven,*
> *Rücksack on back and aureole in pocket,*
> *And stay in Paradisal pubs, and drink*
> *Immortal toasts in old ambrosia,*
> *Fry wings in nectar on the glassy sea,*
> *And build the fire with twigs of amaranth?*'

Here is his farewell to England, in a letter to Miss Nesbitt from the s.s. *Cedric*: 'I arrived solitary on the boat. After it started I went to the office, more to show that I existed than in the dimmest hope of getting anything—and there was stuck up a list called "Unclaimed Mail." (I thought it sounded as if a lot of the Knights who had promised to equip themselves for the Quest of the Holy Grail had missed the train, or married a wife, or overslept, or something.) And at the top of the list "Mr Rupert Brooke."......

'— day. Time is no more. I have been a million years on this boat. I don't know if it's this month or last or next. Sometime, remotely, in a past existence,

I was on land. But this is another existence. . . . I have my joys. Today I ate *clam-chowder*. That's romance, isn't it? I ordered it quite recklessly. I didn't know what it was. I only knew that anything called *clam-chowder* must be strange beyond words.

> '*If you were like clam-chowder*
> *And I were like the spoon,*
> *And the the band were playing louder*
> *And a little more in tune,*
> *I'd stir you till I spilled you,*
> *Or kiss you till I killed you,*
> *If you were like clam-chowder*
> *And I were like the spoon.*

(But you don't know Swinburne.) "Clam-chowder," my God! what am I coming to? . . .

'I haven't told you much about my voyage, have I? There's not much to tell. I felt, before I got your letter, a trifle lonely at Liverpool. Everybody else seemed to have people to see them off. So I went back on shore and found a dirty little boy, who was unoccupied, and said his name was William. "Will you wave to me if I give you sixpence, William?" I said. "Why yes," said William. So I gave him sixpence, and went back on board. And when the time came he leaned over his railing on the landing-stage, and waved. And now and then he shouted indistinct messages in a shrill voice. And as we slid away, the last object I looked at was a small dot waving a white handkerchief, or nearly white, faithfully. So I got my sixpenn'orth and my farewell—Dear William!'

AMERICA

For his travels in America and Canada, his letters to the *Westminster Gazette*, since republished, must be allowed in the main to speak; but these may be supplemented by scraps of his letters to his Mother and his friends. 'America hasn't changed me much yet,' he wrote from New York. 'I've got the adorablest little touch of an American accent, and I'm a bit thinner.' He wasn't very happy at first. 'When I'm alone,' he wrote to me on June 29th from the Montreal Express, 'I sink into a kind of mental stupor which may last for months. I shan't be really right till I get back to you all.' And again from Ottawa, ten days later, 'I don't get very miserable, or go to pieces (save for occasional bursts of home-sickness just before meals); but my whole level of life descends to an incredible muddy flatness. I do no reading, no thinking, no writing. And very often I don't see many things. The real hell of it is that I get so numb that my brain and senses don't record fine or clear impressions. So the time is nearly all waste. I'm very much ashamed of it all. For I've always beforehand a picture of myself dancing through foreign cities, drinking in novelty, hurling off letters to the *W.G.*, breaking into song and sonnet, dashing off plays and novels. . . . Lord, Lord! . . . . . .

'American "hospitality" means that with the nice ones you can be at once on happy and intimate terms. Oh dear, the tears quite literally well up into my eyes when I think of a group of young Harvard people I tumbled into—at Harvard. They had the charm and freshness and capacity for instantly creating a relation

95

of happy and warm friendliness that, for instance, Denis[1] has. It's a nice thing ......

'You, at home, have no conception how you're all getting a sanctity and halo about you in my mind. I dwell so much and so sentimentally on all the dear dead days that I am beginning to see no faults and all virtues in all of you. *You*, my dear, appear perfection in every part. Your passion for anagrams is a lovable and deeply intellectual taste. Your acquaintance with [*a bête noire* of his] a beautiful thing. Your lack of sympathy with the Labour Party turns to a noble and picturesque Toryism. Even your preference for gilded over comfortable chairs loses something of its ugliness in my heart. Of you and Norton and Duncan [Grant] and —— and even —— I think incessantly, devotedly, and tearfully. Even of figures who, to be frank, have hovered but dimly on the outskirts of my consciousness, I am continually and fragrantly memorial. . . .
. . . I make up little minor, pitiful songs, the burden of which is that I have a folk-longing to get back from all this Imperial luxury to the simplicity of the little places and quiet folks I knew and loved. One very beautiful one has the chorus—

'Would God I were eating plover's eggs,
  And drinking dry champagne,
With the Bernard Shaws, Mr and Mrs Masefield, Lady
  Horner, Neil Primrose, Raleigh, the Right Honour-
  able Augustine Birrell, Eddie, six or seven Asquiths,
  and Felicity Tree,
    In Downing Street again.'

  [1] Denis Browne, of whom more hereafter.

96

His next letter was from Toronto, a fortnight later:
'I've found here an Arts and Letters Club of poets.
painters, journalists, etc., where they'd heard of me,
and read G.P.,[1] and, oh Eddie, one fellow actually
possessed my "Poems." Awful Triumph. Every now
and then one comes up and presses my hand and says,
"Wal, Sir, you cannot know what a memorable Day
in my life this is." Then I do my pet boyish-modesty
stunt and go pink all over; and everyone thinks it *too*
delightful. One man said to me, "Mr Brooks"
(my Canadian name), "Sir, I may tell you that in
my opinion you have Mr Noyes skinned." That
means I'm better than him: a great compliment. But
they're really quite an up-to-date lot; and very
cheery and pleasant. I go tomorrow to the desert
and the wilds.'

The desert and the wilds suited him much better
than the cities. 'Today,' he wrote to Miss Nesbitt on
the 3rd of August from Lake George, about 70 miles
from Winnipeg, 'I'm 26 years old—and I've done so
little. I'm very much ashamed. By God, I am going
to make things hum though—but that's all so far
away. I'm lying quite naked on a beach of golden
sand, 6 miles away from the hunting-lodge, the other
man near by, a gun between us in case bears appear,
the boat pulled up on the shore, the lake very blue and
ripply, and the sun rather strong. . . . . . . We caught
two pike on the way out, which lie picturesquely in
the bows of the boat. Along the red-gold beach are
the tracks of various wild animals, mostly jumping-

[1] *Georgian Poetry.*

deer and caribou. One red-deer we saw as we came round the corner, lolloping along the beach, stopping and snuffling the wind, and then going on again. Very lovely. We were up-wind and it didn't see us, and the meat wasn't needed, so we didn't shoot at it (I'm glad, I'm no "sportsman"). We bathed off the beach, and then lit a fire of birch and spruce, and fried eggs, and ate cold caribou-heart, and made tea, and had, oh! blueberry pie. Cooking and eating a meal naked is the most solemnly primitive thing one can do ; and—this is the one thing which will make you realise that I'm living far the most wonderfully and incredibly romantic life you ever heard of, and infinitely superior to your miserable crawling London existence—the place we landed at is an INDIAN CAMP. At any moment a flotilla of birch-bark canoes may sweep round the corner, crowded with Indians, braves and squaws and papooses—and not those lonely half-breeds and stray Indians that speak English, mind you, but the Real Thing! Shades of Fenimore Cooper!'

But he was quite able to cope with civilisation when he got back to it. The next letter is ten days later, from Edmonton: 'I find I'm becoming very thick-skinned and bold, and the complete journalist. I've just been interviewed by a reporter. I fairly crushed him. I just put my cigar in the corner of my mouth, and undid my coat-buttons, and put my thumbs under my arm-pits, and spat, and said, "Say, Kid, this is some town." He asked me a lot of questions to which I didn't know the answers, so I lied. . . . . . .

'Also I am become very good at boarding people. I just enter railway offices and demand free passes as a journalist, and stamp into immense newspaper buildings and say I want to talk for an hour to the Chief Editor, and I can lean across the counter with a cigarette and discuss the Heart with the young lady who sells cigars, newspapers, and stamps. I believe I could do a deal in Real Estate, in the bar, over a John Collins, with a clean-shaven Yankee with a tremulous eyelid and a moist lower lip. In fact, I am a Man.'

He stayed some days at Vancouver, where he wrote his mother a letter which gives me occasion to stand in a very white sheet. 'I'm glad you like the Westminster articles. They're not always very well written, but I think they're the sort of stuff that ought to interest an intelligent *W.G.* reader more than the ordinary travel stuff one sees. I hope they won't annoy people over this side. Canadians and Americans are so touchy. But it's absurd to ladle out indiscriminate praise, as most people do. I heard from Eddie about the proofs. I was very sad at one thing. In my first or second article I had made an American say "You bet your" —which is good American slang. Eddie thought a word was left out and inserted "boots." I only hope the *W.G.* omitted it. I suppose it'll be printed by now. If not, 'phone the *W.G.* or write— But it must be too late. Alas! Alas!

'Vancouver is a queer place, rather different from the rest of Canada. More oriental. The country and harbour are rather beautiful, with great violet mountains all round, snow-peaks in the distance. They interviewed me and put (as usual) a quite inaccurate report of it in the paper, saying I'd come here to investigate the Japanese question. In consequence about five people rang me up every morning at 8 o'clock (British Columbians get up an hour earlier than I) to say they wanted to wait on me and give me their views. Out here they always have telephones in the bedrooms. One old sea-captain came miles to tell me that the Japanese—and every other—trouble was due to the fact that British Columbia had neglected the teaching of the Gospels on the land question. He wasn't so far out in some respects.'

He sailed for Hawaii from San Francisco, where he was warmly welcomed at Berkeley University by Professor Gayly and Professor Wells, and made many friends among the undergraduates. 'California,' he wrote to me on the 1st of October, 'is nice, and the Californians a friendly bunch. There's a sort of goldenness about 'Frisco and the neighbourhood. It hangs in the air, and about the people. Everyone is very cheery and cordial and simple. They are rather a nation apart, different from the rest of the States. Much more like the English. As everywhere in this extraordinary country, I am welcomed with open arms when I say I know Masefield and Goldie![1] It's very queer. I can't for the life of me help moving about like a metropolitan among rustics, or an Athenian in Thrace. Their wide-mouthed awe at England is so touching —they really are a colony of ours still. That they

[1] G. Lowes Dickinson.

should be speaking to a man who knows Lowes
Dickinson, has met Galsworthy, who once saw Belloc
plain!... What should we feel if we could speak with
an *habitué* of the theatre at Athens, Fifth Century, or
with Mine Host of the Mermaid? All that they have
with me, the dears! Yet I don't know why I write
this from California, the one place that has a literature
and tradition of its own.

'On Tuesday—the Pacific. I'll write thence, but God
knows when it'll get to you.'

He wrote nothing to the *Westminster* about the
South Seas. He had got a letter from which he at first
inferred, quite wrongly, that only one series of articles
was wanted from him. 'Isn't it beastly?' he wrote. 'I
supposed I was going on once a week for months and
and years. I could read me once a week for ever,
couldn't you?' Further correspondence cleared up the
misunderstanding, and the real reason for his silence
must have been that he found the life of the islands too
absorbing. But there are plenty of letters to friends.
'The Pacific,' he wrote from the steamer on October
12th, 'has been very pacific, God be thanked—so
I've had a pleasant voyage. Three passionate Pacific
women cast lustrous eyes towards me, but, with a dim
remembrance of the fate of Conrad characters who
succumbed to such advances, I evade them. I pass my
hand wearily through my long hair, and say, "Is not
the soul of Maurya a glimmering wing in the moth-
hour?" or words to that effect. The Celtic method is
not understood in this part of the world.'

The first stop was at Honolulu, where he stayed on

Waikiki beach, the scene of the sonnet beginning 'Warm perfumes like a breath from vine and tree.' He wrote to his Mother without enthusiasm: 'Honolulu itself is a dreadfully American place, just like any city in the States or Canada'; and he found little better to say of the country round about than that 'it really *is* tropical in character, like some of the gardens and places at Cannes, on an immense scale.'

But this is what he wrote to me about Samoa from the steamer taking him to Fiji: 'It's all true about the South Seas! I get a little tired of it at moments, because I am just too old for Romance. But there it is; there it wonderfully is; heaven on earth, the ideal life, little work, dancing and singing and eating; naked people of incredible loveliness, perfect manners, and immense kindliness, a divine tropic climate, and intoxicating beauty of scenery. I wandered with an "interpreter"—entirely genial and quite incapable of English—through Samoan villages. The last few days I stopped in one, where a big marriage feast was going on. I lived in a Samoan house (the coolest in the world) with a man and his wife, nine children ranging from a proud beauty of 18 to a round object of 1 year, a god, a cat, a proud hysterical hen, and a gaudy scarlet and green parrot who roved the roof and beams with a wicked eye, choosing a place whence to —— twice a day, with humorous precision, on my hat and clothes.

'The Samoan girls have extraordinarily beautiful bodies, and walk like goddesses. They're a lovely brown colour, without any black Melanesian admixture. Can't you imagine how shattered and fragmen-

tary a heart I'm bearing away to Fiji and Tahiti? And,
oh dear! I'm afraid they'll be just as bad.

'And it's all true about, for instance, cocoanuts. You
tramp through a strange, vast, dripping, tropical
forest for hours, listening to weird liquid hootings
from birds and demons in the branches above. Then
you feel thirsty. So you send your boy up a great perpendicular palm. He runs up with utter ease and grace,
cuts off a couple of vast nuts, and comes down and
makes holes in them. And they're chock-full of the
best drink in the world. Romance! Romance! I
walked 15 miles through mud and up and down
mountains, and swam three rivers, to get this boat.
But if ever you miss me, suddenly, one day, from lec-
ture-room B in King's, or from the Moulin d'Or at
lunch, you'll know that I've got sick for the full moon
on these little thatched roofs, and the palms against
the morning, and the Samoan boys and girls diving
thirty feet into a green sea or a deep mountain pool
under a waterfall—and that I've gone back.'

The next place was Fiji, where he wrote to Edmund
Gosse from Suva on November 19th. 'I've just got
into this place, from Samoa. I said to myself, "Fiji is
obviously the wildest place I can get to round here.
The name, and pictures of the inhabitants, prove it,"
And lo! a large English town, with two banks, several
churches, dental surgeons, a large gaol, auctioneers,
bookmakers, two newspapers, and all the other appur-
tenances of civilisation! But I fancy I'll be able to get
some little boat and go off to some smaller wilder
islands. . . . . . .

'Perplexing country! At home everything is so simple, and choice is swift, for the sensible man. There is only the choice between writing a good sonnet and making a million pounds. Who could hesitate? But *here* the choice is between writing a sonnet, and climbing a straight hundred-foot cocoanut palm, or diving forty feet from a rock into pellucid blue-green water. Which is the better, there? One's European literary soul begins to be haunted by strange doubts and shaken with fundamental, fantastic misgivings. I think I shall return home. . . . . . .

'Oh, it's horribly true, what you wrote, that one only finds in the South Seas what one brings there. Perhaps I could have found Romance if I'd brought it. Yet I do not think one could help but find *less* trouble than one brings. The idea of the South Seas as a place of passion and a Mohammedan's paradise is but a sailor's yarn. It is nothing near so disturbing. It's rather the opposite of alcohol according to the Porter's definition: for it promotes performance but takes away desire. Yet I can understand Stevenson finding—as you put it—the Shorter Catechism there. One keeps realising, however unwillingly, responsibility. I noticed in myself, and in the other white people in Samoa, a trait that I have remarked in Schoolmasters. You know that sort of slightly irritated tolerance, and lack of *irresponsibility*, that mark the pedagogue? One feels that one's a White Man (*vide* Kipling *passim*)—ludicrously. I kept thinking I was in the Sixth at Rugby again. These dear good people, with their laughter and friendliness and

crowns of flowers one feels that one must protect
them. If one was having an evening out with Falstaff
and Bardolph themselves, and a small delightful child
came up with "Please I'm lost and I want to get
home," wouldn't one have to leave good fellowship
and spend the evening in mean streets tracking its
abode. That's, I fancy, how the white man feels in
these forgotten—and dissolving—pieces of heaven.
And that perhaps is what Stevenson felt—I don't
know enough about him. His memory is sweet there,
in Samoa; especially among the natives. The white
men, mostly traders, who remain from his time, have
—for such people—very warm recollections of his personality; but—with a touch of pathos—avow themselves unable to see any merit in his work. Such stuff
as the *Wrong Box* they frankly can't understand a
grown man writing . . . I went up the steep hill
above Vailima, where the grave is. It's a high and
lonely spot. I took a Samoan of about 20 to guide me.
He was much impressed by Stevenson's fame. "That
fellow," he said, "I think every fellow in world know
him." Then he looked perplexed. "But my father
say," he went on, "Stevenson no big man—small
man." That a slight man of medium height should be
so famous, puzzled him altogether. If he had been
seven feet high, now! Fame is a curious thing.......
Oh, *do* forgive the envelope. My own, in this awful
climate, are all fast stuck, though never filled, like an
English churchman's mind. And I'm reduced to these
fantastic affairs.'

Other letters add touches to his picture. To me he

wrote: 'Suva is a queer place; much civilised; full of English people who observe the Rules of Etiquette, and call on third Thursdays, and do not speak to the "natives." Fiji's not so attractive as Samoa, but more *macabre*. Across the bay are ranges of inky, sinister mountains, over which there are always clouds and darkness. No matter how fine or windy or hot or cheerful it may be in Suva, that trans-sinutic region is nothing but forbidding and terrible. The Greeks would have made it the entrance to the other world— it is just what I've always imagined Avernus to be like. I'm irresistibly attracted by them, and when I come back from my cruise, I intend to walk among them. Shall I return? If not, spill some blood in a trench—you'll find the recipe in Homer—and my wandering shade will come for an hour or two to lap it. . . . . . . The sunsets here! the colour of the water over the reef! the gloom and terror of those twisted mountains! and the extraordinary contrasts in the streets and the near country—for there are fifty thousand Hindoos, indentured labour, here, emaciated, and proud, in Liberty-coloured garments, mournful, standing out among these gay, pathetic, sturdy children the Fijians. The Hindoos, who were civilised when we were Fijians; and the Fijians, who will never be civilised. And amongst them, weedy Australian clerks, uncertain whether they most despise a "haw-haw Englishman" or a "dam nigger," and without the conscience of the one or the charm of the other; secret devil-worshippers, admirers of America, English without tradition and Yankees without go. Give

me a landed gentry, ten shillings on wheat, and hang-
ing for sheep-stealing; also the Established Church,
whence I spring.'

To Denis Browne he wrote about the dancing and
the music: 'I prefer watching a *Siva-Siva* to observing
Nijinsky. Oh dear, I so wish you'd been with me for
some of these native dances. I've got no ear, and can't
get the tunes down. They're very simple—just a few
bars with a scale of about 5 notes, repeated over and
over again. But it's the *Rhythm* that gets you. They
get extraordinarily rhythmic effects, everybody beating their hands, or tapping with a stick; and the
dancers swaying their bodies and tapping with their
feet. None of that damned bounding and pirouetting.
Just *stylisierte* pantomime, sometimes slightly in-
decent. But *most* exciting. Next time I get sick of England, I'm going to bring you along out here, and
work the whole thing out.

'You won't know me when—if ever—I return.
Many things I have lost; my knowledge of art and
literature, my fragmentary manners, my acquaintance
with the English tongue, and any slight intelligence I
ever had; but I have gained other things; a rich red-
brown for my skin, a knowledge of mixed drinks, an
ability to talk or drink with any kind of man, and a
large *repertoire* of dirty stories. Am I richer or poorer?
I don't know. I only regret that I shall never be able to
mix in your or any intelligent circles again. I am indistinguishable (except by my poverty) from a Hall man.'

'Dear Miss Asquith,'[1] he wrote in mid-December

[1] Now Lady Violet Bonham-Carter.

from 'somewhere in the mountains of Fiji,' 'Forgive this paper. Its limpness is because it has been in terrific thunderstorms, and through most of the rivers in Fiji, in the last few days. Its marks of dirt are because small naked brown babies *will* crawl up and handle it. *And any blood-stains will be mine.* The point is, will they ...? It's absurd, I know. It's twenty years since they've eaten anybody, and far more since they've done what I particularly and unreasonably detest—fastened the victim down, cut pieces off him one by one, and cooked and eaten them before his eyes. To witness one's own transubstantiation into a naked black man, that seems the last indignity. Consideration of the thoughts that pour through the mind of the ever-diminishing remnant of a man, as it sees its late limbs cooking, move me deeply. I have been meditating a sonnet, as I sit here, surrounded by dusky faces and gleaming eyes:

> '*Dear, they have poached the eyes you loved so well*—

It'd do well for No. 101 and last, in a modern sonnet-sequence, wouldn't it? I don't know how it would go on. The fourth line would have to be

> '*And all my turbulent lips are* maître-d'hotel—

I don't know how to scan French. I fancy that limps. But "*all*" is very strong in the modern style.
  'The idea comes out in a slighter thing:

> '*The limbs that erstwhile charmed your sight*
> *Are now a savage's delight;*

FIJI

The ear that heard your whispered vow
Is one of many entrées now—
Broiled are the arms in which you clung,
And devilled is the angelic tongue: . . .
And oh! my anguish as I see
A Black Man gnaw your favourite knee!
Of the two eyes that were your ruin,
One now observes the other stewing.
My lips (the inconstancy of man!)
Are yours no more. The legs that ran
Each dewy morn their love to wake,
Are now a steak, are now a steak! . . .

Oh, dear! I suppose it ought to end on the Higher
Note, the Wider Outlook. Poetry has to, they tell
me. You may caress details, all the main parts of the
poem, but at last you have to open the window and turn
to God, or Earth, or Eternity, or any of the Grand Old
Endings. It gives Uplift, as we Americans say. And
that's so essential. (Did you ever notice how the
Browning family's poems all refer suddenly to God
in the last line? It's laughable if you read through
them in that way. "What if that friend happened to
be—God?" "What comes next? Is it—God?" "And
with God be the rest." "And if God choose, I shall
but love thee better after death.". . . etc. etc. I forget
them all now. It shows what the Victorians were.)
   'So must I soar:

> *'O love, O loveliest and best,*
> *Natives this body may digest;*

Whole, and still yours, my soul *shall dwell,*
Uneaten, safe, incoctible . . .

It's too dull. I shall go out and wander through the
forest paths by the grey moonlight. Fiji in moonlight
is like nothing else in this world or the next. It's all
dim colours and all scents. And here, where it's high
up, the most fantastically shaped mountains in the
world tower up all around, and little silver clouds and
wisps of mist run bleating up and down the valleys
and hillsides like lambs looking for their mother.
There's only one thing on earth as beautiful; and
that's Samoa by moonlight. That's utterly different,
merely Heaven, sheer loveliness. You lie on a mat in
a cool Samoan hut, and look out on the white sand
under the high palms, and a gentle sea, and the black
line of the reef a mile out, and moonlight over everything, floods and floods of it, not sticky, like Honolulu
moonlight, not to be eaten with a spoon, but flat and
abundant, such that you could slice thin golden-white
shavings off it, as off cheese. And then among it all are
the loveliest people in the world, moving and dancing
like gods and goddesses, very quietly and mysteriously, and utterly content. It is sheer beauty, so pure
that it's difficult to breathe in it—like living in a Keats
world, only it's less syrupy—Endymion without sugar.
Completely unconnected with this world.
'There is a poem:

'*I know an Island*
Where the long scented holy nights pass slow,
And there, 'twixt lowland and highland,

FIJI

The white stream falls into a pool I know
Deep, hidden with ferns and flowers, soft as dreaming,
Where the brown laughing dancing bathers go . . .

'It ends, after many pages:

'I know an Island
Where the slow fragrant-breathing nights creep past;
And there, 'twixt lowland and highland,
A deep, fern-shrouded, murmurous water glimmers;
There I'll come back at last,
And find my friends, the flower-crowned, laughing
    swimmers,
And—[1]

'I forget. And I've not written the middle part. And it's very bad, like all true poems. I love England; and all the people in it; but oh, how can one know of heaven on earth and not come back to it? I'm afraid I shall slip away from that slithery, murky place you're (I suppose) in now, and return— Ridiculous.

'I continue in a hot noon, under an orange tree. We rose at dawn and walked many miles and swam seven large rivers and picked and ate many oranges and pineapples and drank cocoanuts. Now the two "boys" who carry my luggage are asleep in the shade. They're Fijians of twenty-three or so who know a few words of English. One of them is the finest-made man I've ever seen; like a Greek statue come to life; strong as ten horses. To see him strip and swim a half-flooded river is an immortal sight.

[1] These lines appear again, considerably altered, in the essay called *Some Niggers*, printed in *Letters from America*.

'Last night we stayed in the house of a mountain chief who has spasmodic yearnings after civilisation. When these grow strong, he sends a runner down to the coast to buy any illustrated papers he can find. He knows no English, but he pastes his favourite pictures up round the wall and muses over them. I lectured on them —fragments of the *Sketch* and *Sphere* for several years —to a half-naked reverent audience last night (through my interpreter of course). The Prince of Wales, looking like an Oxford undergraduate, elbows two ladies who display 1911 spring-fashions. A golf champion in a most contorted position occupies a central place. He is regarded, I fancy, as a rather potent and violent deity. To his left is "Miss Viola Tree, as Eurydice," to his right Miss Lillah M'Carthy as Jocasta, looking infinitely Mycenaean. I explained about incest, shortly, and Miss M'C. rose tremendously in Fijian estimation. Why do people like their gods to be so eccentric, always? I fancy I left an impression that she was Mr H. H. Hilton's (is that right? You're a golfer) mother and wife. It is so hard to explain our civilisation to simple people. Anyhow, I disturbed their theology and elevated Lillah to the top place. How Eurydice came in puzzled them and me. I fancy they regard her as a Holy Ghostess, in some sort.

'It's very perplexing. These people—Samoans and Fijians—are so much nicer, and so *much* better-mannered, than oneself. They are stronger, beautifuller, kindlier, more hospitable and courteous, greater lovers of beauty, and even wittier, than average Europeans. And they are—under our influence—a dying race.

We gradually fill their lands with plantations and Indian coolies. The Hawaiians, up in the Sandwich Islands, have almost altogether gone, and their arts and music with them, and their islands are a replica of America. A cheerful thought, that all these places are to become indistinguishable from Denver and Birmingham and Stuttgart, and the people of dress and behaviour precisely like Herr Schmidt, and Mr Robinson, and Hiram O. Guggenheim. And now they're so . . . it's impossible to describe how far nearer the Kingdom of Heaven—or the Garden of Eden—these good, naked, laughing people are than oneself or one's friends. . . . But I forget. You are an anti-socialist, and I mustn't say a word against our modern industrial system. I beg your pardon.

'I go down to the coast to catch a boat to New Zealand, where I shall post this. Thence to Tahiti, to hunt for lost Gauguins. Then back to barbarism in America. God knows when I shall get home. In the spring, I hope. Is England still there? Forgive this endless scrawl.

'I suppose you're rushing from lunch-party to lunch-party, and dance to dance, and opera to political platform. Won't you come and learn how to make a hibiscus-wreath for your hair, and sail a canoe, and swim two minutes under water catching turtles, and dive forty feet into a waterfall, and climb a cocoanut-palm? It's more worth while.'

Sometimes the desire for England and his friends came uppermost. 'I'd once thought it necessary to marry,' he wrote to Jacques Raverat from Fiji. 'I *approve* of marriage for the world. I think you're all quite right, so don't be alarmed. But not for me. I'm too old. The Point of Marriage is Peace—to work in. But can't one get it otherwise? Why, certainly, when one's old. And so I will. I know what things are good: friendship and work and conversation. These I shall have. How one can fill life, if one's energetic and knows how to dig! I have thought of a thousand things to do, in books and poems and plays and theatres and societies and housebuilding and dinner-parties, when I get Home. We shall have fun. Now we have so painfully achieved middle-age, shall we not reap the fruits of that achievement, my dyspeptic friend? By God, yes! Will you come and walk with me in Spain next summer? And will you join me on the Poet's Round?—a walk I've planned. One starts from Charing Cross, in a south-easterly direction, and calls on de la Mare at Anerley, and finds Davies at Sevenoaks—a day's march to Belloc at King's Land, then up to Wibson[1] on the borders of Gloucester-shire, back by Stratford, RUGBY, and the Chilterns, where Masefield and Chesterton dwell. Wouldn't it give one a queer idea of England?

'Three months a year I am going to live with you and Gwen, three with Dudley and Anne, three with the Ranee,[2] and three alone. A perfect life. I almost catch the next boat to 'Frisco at the thought of it.' (At this point in the letter there is a constellation of blots, explained as 'Tears of Memory.')

'There is nothing in the world like friendship. And

[1] Wilfrid Gibson. [2] His name for his mother.

there is no man who has had such friends as I, so many, so fine, so various, so multiform, so prone to laughter, so strong in affection, and so permanent, so trustworthy, so courteous, so stern with vices and so blind to faults or folly, of such swiftness of mind and strength of body, so apt both to make jokes and to understand them. Also their faces are beautiful, and I love them. I repeat a long list of their names every night before I sleep. Friendship is always exciting, and yet always safe. There is no lust in it, and therefore no poison. It is cleaner than love, and older; for children and very old people have friends, but they do not love. It gives more and takes less, it is fine in the enjoying, and without pain when absent, and it leaves only good memories. In love all laughter ends with an ache, but laughter is the very garland on the head of friendship. I will not love, and I will not be loved. But I will have friends round me continually, all the days of my life, and in whatever lands I may be. So we shall laugh and eat and sing, and go great journeys in boats and on foot, and write plays and perform them, and pass innumerable laws taking their money from the rich. . . . I err. I praise too extravagantly, conveying an impression that friendship always gives peace. And even at the moment I feel a hunger, too rending for complete peace, to see all your faces again and to eat food with you.'

Home thoughts from abroad of a different order were sent to Miss Nesbitt: 'I see I'm going to have the hell of an uncomfortable life,' he wrote. 'I want too many different things. I keep now pining after

London. I want to talk, talk, talk. Is there anything better in the world than sitting at a table and eating good food and drinking great drink, and discussing everything under the sun with wise and brilliant people?......

'Oh but I'm going to have such a time when I get back. I'm going to have the loveliest rooms in King's, and I'm going to spend 5 days a week there, and 3 in London (that's 8, stoopid), and in King's I'm going to entertain all the mad and lovely people in the world, and I'm never going to sit down to dinner without a philosopher, a poet, a musician, an actress, a dancer, and a bishop at table with me. I'm going to get up such performances as will turn Cambridge upside down. I'm going to have Yeats and Cannan and Craig and Barker to give a lecture each on modern drama. I'm going to have my great play in the Grantchester garden. I'm going—oh, hell, I don't know what I'm going to do—but every morning I shall drift up and down the backs in a punt, discussing anything in the world with anybody who desires.'

He left Fiji in December. 'Life's been getting madder and madder,' he wrote from Auckland on December 17th. 'I tumbled into Fiji without a friend or an introduction, and left it a month later amidst the loud grief of the united population, white and black. The two "boys" (aged 23 or 24) I took with me when I went walking through the centre of the island, to carry my bags, are my sworn and eternal friends. One of them ("Ambele," under which I, but not you, can recognise "Abel") was six foot high, very broad, and more perfectly made than any man or statue I have ever seen. His grin stretched from ear to ear. And he could carry me across rivers (when I was tired of swimming them, for we crossed vast rivers every mile or two) for a hundred yards or so, as I should carry a box of matches. I think of bringing him back with me as a servant or bodyguard to England. He loved me because, though I was far weaker than he, I was far braver. The Fijians are rather cowards. And on precipices I am peculiarly reckless. The boys saved me from rolling off to perdition about thirty times, and respected me for it, though thinking me insane. What would you say if I turned up with two vast cannibal servants, black-skinned and perpetually laughing—all of us attired only in loin-cloths, and red flowers in our hair? I think I should be irresistible.

'Why, precisely, I'm here, I don't know. I seem to have missed a boat somewhere, and I can't get on to Tahiti till the beginning of January. Damn. And I hear that a man got to Tahiti two months ahead of me, and found—and carried off—some Gauguin paintings on glass. DAMN!

'New Zealand turns out to be in the midst of summer, and almost exactly like England. I eat strawberries, large garden strawberries, every day; and it's the middle of December! It feels curiously unnatural, perverse, like some frightful vice out of Havelock Ellis. I blush and eat secretively.

'I'll describe New Zealand another day. It's a sort of Fabian England, very upper-middle-class and gentle and happy (after Canada), no poor, and the Government owning hotels and running char-à-bancs. All the women smoke, and dress very badly, and nobody drinks. Everybody seems rather ugly—but perhaps that's compared with the South Seas.'

The Englishness of New Zealand made home affairs vivid to him again, and he wrote vehemently to his mother about the Dublin Strike. 'I feel wild about Dublin. I always feel in strikes that "the men are always right," as a man says in *Clayhanger*. Of course the poor are always right against the rich, though often enough the men are in the wrong over some point of the moment (it's not to be wondered at). But Dublin seems to be one of the clearest cases on record....... When the *Times* begins saying that the employers are in the wrong, they must be very unpardonably and rottenly so indeed. I do hope people are contributing for the wives and children in Dublin. Could you send two guineas in my name? I'll settle when I get back. But I'd like it done immediately. I expect you will have sent some yourself.'......

'The queer thing [about New Zealand],' he goes on, 'is that they've got all the things in the Liberal or mild Fabian programme:—eight hour day (and less), bigger old age pensions, access to the land, minimum wage, insurance, etc. etc., and yet it's not Paradise. The same troubles exist in much the same form (except that there's not much bad poverty). Cost of living is rising quicker than wages. There are the same troubles between unions and employers, and between rich and poor. I suppose there'll be no peace anywhere till the rich are curbed altogether.'

On the voyage from New Zealand to Tahiti he made great friends with a Lancashire business man, Mr Harold Ashworth, who wrote after his death to Mrs Brooke. The letters show the kind of impression that he made on those who met him at this time. 'I am happy to believe,' says Mr Ashworth, 'that he and I became real friends, and many a time I would invoke his aid when my rather aggressive Radicalism brought the "Smoke-room" men at me *en masse*. I never met so entirely likeable a chap, and when I could "get him going" about his wanderings, or provoke him into discussions about Literature, I was one walking ear! ...... I almost wept to know I could never again see that golden head and kindly smile—"Young Apollo," I used to dub him in my mind, whilst the fresh wind tossed his hair, and his boyish eyes lit up with pleasure at some of my anecdotes of strange people and places. ...... Your son was not merely a genius; what is perhaps more important, he had a charm that was literally like Sunshine. To say his manner was *perfect* is putting it quite inadequately. .... His memory is blessed by hundreds of men like me who were so fortunate as to meet him and were the better for that happy adventure.'

Another friend made on his travels was Reginald Berkeley, who was his chief companion on his excursions in Fiji. Rupert sent him from the s.s. *Niagara* a long letter about the technique of writing. 'One can only advise people two or three years younger,' he says, 'Beyond that, one has forgotten.' The end of it shows him insisting on the importance for artists of the attitude which he had recommended for everyone in his letter to Ben Keeling of three years before. 'Finally,' he says, 'I charge you, be kind to life; and do not bruise her with the bludgeon of the *a priori*. Poor dirty woman, she responds to sympathy. Sympathetic imagination with everybody and everything is the artist's one duty. He should be one with every little clergyman, and the stockbroker's most secret hope should be his hope. In the end, the words of Strindberg's heroine are the only motto, "The race of man is greatly to be pitied." Isn't that true? Hatred should be given out sparingly. It's too valuable to use carelessly. And, misused, it prevents understanding. And it is our duty to understand; for if we don't, no one else will.'

His next stay was about three months in Tahiti. 'I've decided to stay here another month,' he wrote to Miss Nesbitt in February, 'for two very good reasons: (1) that I haven't enough money to get out, (2) that I've found the most ideal place in the world to live and work in.[1] A wide verandah over a blue lagoon, a wooden pier with deep clear water for diving, and coloured fish that swim between your toes. There also swim between your toes, more or less, scores of laughing brown babies from two years to fourteen. Canoes and boats, rivers, fishing with spear, net and line, the

[1] This was at Mataiea, about 30 miles from the chief town, Papeete.

most wonderful food in the world strange fishes and vegetables perfectly cooked. Europe slides from me terrifyingly. . . . . . . Will it come to your having to fetch me? The boat's ready to start; the brown lovely people in their bright clothes are gathered on the old wharf to wave her away. Everyone has a white flower behind their ear. Mamua has given me one. Do you know the significance of a white flower worn over the ear? A white flower over the right ear means "I am looking for a sweetheart." And a white flower over the left ear means "I have found a sweetheart." And a white flower over each ear means "I have one sweetheart, and am looking for another." A white flower over each ear, my dear, is dreadfully the most fashionable way of adorning yourself in Tahiti.

'*Bon voyage* to the travellers. Good luck to everybody else. Love to the whole world. Tonight we will put scarlet flowers in our hair, and sing strange slumbrous South Sea songs to the concertina, and drink red French wine, and dance, and bathe in a soft lagoon by moonlight, and eat great squelchy tropical fruits, custard-apples, papaia, pomegranate, mango, guava and the rest. *Urana*. I have a million lovely and exciting things to tell you—but not now.'

How thoroughly he became imbued with the life, the feeling, and the philosophy of the islands appears from a sociological epistle which he wrote to Jacques Raverat after his return to England. 'As for Land, my Frog, we must have a great deal held in common. It is good for men to work *of* themselves, but not too much *for* themselves. In my part of the world, if we want to build a canoe, we all put wreaths in our hair, and take the town hatchet, and Bill's axe, and each his own hunting-knife, and have a bit of pig each for luck, and a drink, and go out. And as we go we sing. And when we have got to a large tree we sit round it. And the two biggest men take the axes and hit the tree in turn. And the rest of us beat our hands rhythmically and sing a song saying "That is a tree—cut down the tree—we will make a boat," and so on. And when those two are tired, they drink and sit, and other two take their places . . . and later the hollowing of the canoe, and the fashioning of an out-rigger, and the making of benches and the shaping of paddles. And when all's done, we go home and sing all night, and dance a great deal. For we have another canoe.

'And when you have got a lot of other Goddites together, and started to build a Cathedral, why, you'll see what fun it is working together, instead of in a dirty little corner alone, suspicious, greedy, competitive, hating all the world, like a modern artist or a French peasant or a money-lender or a golfer.'

He had begun writing verse again, and in the 'wide verandah' he wrote or finished *Tiare Tahiti*,[1] *Retrospect*, and the *Great Lover*,[2] which he sent me (he had

[1] A postscript to a letter to his mother elucidates a line in this poem. 'They call me *Pupure* here—it means "fair" in Tahitian—because I have fair hair!'

[2] Speculation has been aroused by the line in this poem praising 'the comfortable smell of friendly fingers.' When asked *whose* fingers, he said his nurse's; and admitted that it might have been the soap.

appointed me his 'literary agent or gross-executor' during his travels)[1] for *New Numbers*. This publication had been planned in July by correspondence with Lascelles Abercrombie, John Drinkwater and Wilfrid Gibson. They meant at first to call it *The Gallows Garland*, after The Gallows, Abercrombie's cottage in Gloucestershire, from which it was to be published; and Rupert thought the change very stupid. He had sketched the contents of the first number. Abercrombie was to contribute a short epic, *Asshurbanipal and Nebuchadnezzar*, Drinkwater an ode called *The Sonority of God*, and Gibson two narrative poems, *Poor Bloody Bill* and *The Brave Poor Thing*, from a series named *Gas-Stoves*. Rupert himself did not expect to manage more than one sonnet, to be entitled *Oh dear! Oh dear!* The first number came out in February 1914; and after three more issues it was discontinued because of the war, before his death had broken the fair companionship.

To illustrate his method of work at this time, it may be of interest to print the first draft of the *Psychical Research* sonnet, with his corrections:

> , when we're beyond the sun,
> *Not with vain tears we'll beat, when all is done,*

[1] He took large views of my duties. 'Damn it,' he had written from Vancouver, 'what's the good of a friend if he can't sit down and write off a few poems for one at a pinch? That's what I count on your doing, if the editors press.' I hope this note will not start a vain hunt for *spuria* among the published poems.

MEMOIR

We'll beat
Unheard on the substantial doors, nor tread
                              aimless
Those dusty high-roads of the wandering Dead

Plaintive for Earth; but rather turn and run
Remembering Earth. We'll turn, I think, and run
Down some close-covered by-way of the air,

Some
Or low sweet alley between wind and wind,

Stoop under faint gleams, thread the shadows, find
Pull down the shadows over us, and find

Some
A whispering ghost-forgotten nook, and there
Spend in pure converse our eternal day;
Think each in each, immediately wise;
Learn all we lacked before, hear, know, and say
What this tumultuous body now denies;
And feel, who have laid our groping hands away;
And see, no longer blinded by our eyes.[1]

[1] Though there are no changes in the concluding lines, I
print them for the sake of a parallel, shown me by John Drinkwater, in Andrew Marvell's *Dialogue between Soul and Body,*
where Soul says:
> '*O, who shall from this dungeon raise*
> *A soul enslaved so many ways,*
> *With bolts of bones, that fettered stands*
> *In feet, and manacled in hands;*
> *Here blinded with an eye, and there*
> *Deaf with the drumming of an ear?*'

But to return to Tahiti. 'I've been ill,' he wrote to me on March 7th. 'I got some beastly coral-poisoning into my legs, and a local microbe on the top of that, and made the places worse by neglecting them, and sea-bathing all day (which turns out to be the worst possible thing). I was in the country when it came on bad, and tried native remedies, which took all the skin off, and produced such a ghastly appearance that I hurried into town. . . . . . . I've got over it now, and feel very spry. I'm in a hovel at the back of the hotel, and contemplate the yard. The extraordinary life of the place flows round and through my room—for here no one, man or woman, scruples to come through one's room at any moment, if it happens to be a short cut. By day nothing much happens in the yard—except when a horse tried to eat a hen the other afternoon. But by night, after ten, it's filled with flitting figures of girls, with wreaths of white flowers, keeping assignations. Occasionally two rivals meet, and fill the darker corners with cursings and scratchings. Or occasionally a youth intercepts a faithless lady, and has a pretty operatic scene under my window. It is all —all Papeete—like a Renaissance Italy, with the venom taken out. No, simpler, light-come and light-go, passionate and forgetful, like children, and all the time South Pacific, that is to say unmalicious and good-tempered. . . . . . .

'I really do feel a little anchorless. I shall be glad to be back among you all, and tied to somewhere in England. I'll never, never, never go to sea again. All I want in life is a cottage, and leisure to write supreme poems and plays. I can't do it in this vagabondage.'

I don't know what happened between this letter and the next to produce the gloom it shows about his work. He had always, at school and onwards, been apt to have fits of thinking that he would never write again, but this time the foreboding seems more serious than usual. He begins cheerfully 'some time in March': 'It's *so* funny; getting a letter of January 25, and not having heard anything from anybody since October. Your letter of November, announcing your marriage with [someone very improbable]; your kindly Christmas information about the disastrous fire in Bilton Road and the disposal of the Ranee's and Alfred's cinders; your New Year's epistle announcing your, Wilfrid's and Albert's Knighthoods; the later letter that recounted your conversations with Shaw, the Earthquake, the War with Germany, the Chinese Ballet, Stravinsky's comic opera, the new El Greco. Gilbert [Cannan]'s trial, Masefield's latest knockabout farce, Arthur Benson's duel . . . all these I have not yet had. They await me in 'Frisco. So I take up the threads at the 25th of January—now itself some way down in the heap of yesterday's seven thousand years—and study them rather confusedly. Flecker—Wilfrid—poetry—plays—Moulin d'Or—*Hullo Tango!* they all stir, these names, some dusty memories away in the back of my subconsciousness. Somewhere they must have meant something to me, in another life. A vision of taxis slides across the orange and green of the sunset. For a moment the palms dwindle to lamp-posts.

TAHITI

'*So a poor ghost beside his misty streams*
Is haunted by strange doubts and fugitive dreams,
Hints of a pre-Lethean life, of men,
Rocks, stars, and skin, things unintelligible,
And the sun on waving grass—he knows not when,
And feet that ran, but where, he cannot tell.[1]

'(You recognise the master-hand?)

'I must come back and see if I can take to it again.
Plan out a life for me for next year, Eddie. (Here follows another sketch for living at Cambridge, much
the same as the one already given.) The other half of
the week I shall reside with you—I warn you.

'But, my dear, I doubt if you'll have me. The Game
is Up, Eddie. If I've gained facts through knocking
about with Conrad characters in a Gauguin *entourage*,
—I've lost a dream or two. I tried to be a poet. And
because I'm a clever writer, and because I was forty
times as sensitive as anybody else, I succeeded a little.
Es ist vorüber; es ist unwiederruflich zu Ende. I am what
I came out here to be. Hard, quite quite hard. I have
become merely a minor character in a Kipling story.

'I'll never be able to write anything more, I think;
or perhaps I can do plays of a sort. . . . I think I'll have
to manage a theatre. I feel very energetic; and very
capable. Is that a great come-down? I think that what
I really feel like is living. I want to talk and talk and
talk . . . and in the intervals have extraordinary adventures. Perhaps this, too, is a come-down. But haven't
I, at 26, reached the age when one should begin to

[1] An unrevised form of part of the sonnet *Hauntings*.

127

learn? An energy that had rushed on me with the cessation of my leprous skin-disease, and the approaching end of six months' peace of soul, is driving me furiously on. This afternoon I go fishing in a canoe with a native girl on a green and purple reef. Tonight from ten to two, spearing fish in the same lagoon by torchlight. Tomorrow at dawn, up into the mountains on foot with a mad Englishman, four natives, and a half-caste, to a volcanic lake in the interior. There we build a house and stay for two days. The natives return, and the M.E. and myself push on for and pass down to the other coast. Perhaps we get it. Perhaps not.

'In any case we hope to see some ghosts—they abound in the interior. They come to you by night, and as you watch them their bellies burst, and their entrails fall to the ground, and their eyes—unpupilled balls of white—fall out too, and they stink and shine. This morning I've been reading *The Triumph of Time*, and *Bartholomew Fair*. . . . . . .

'Learning, learning, learning. . . . Is there anything else to do except *taste*? Will you come with me to Morocco, Persia, Russia, Egypt, Abyssinia, and the Aran Islands? I'm afraid I shan't be able to settle down at home. It'll be an advantage that I can come to England through America. For then I'll find it so lovely that I won't be hankering after sunlight and brown people and rainbow-coloured fish. At least, I won't for some months, or a year.

'I'll learn at home, a bit. There's so much to learn there—if only one's sensible enough to know it. And

I feel hard enough to make the attempt. I want to
love my friends and hate my enemies, again. Both
greatly—but not *too* much. Which brings me round
to [an enemy] and Clubs.......I want a club to take
an occasional stranger into for a drink, and to read
the papers in, and sometimes to have a quiet meal in.
Where do you think I should go? I want somewhere
I needn't always be spick and span in, and somewhere
I don't have to pay a vast sum. Alas, why are there no
decent clubs? What do the jolly people all do? I want
to belong to the same club as de la Mare. Where does
de la Mare go? To Anerley, S.E., I suppose.

> '*There was once an a-metrist of Anerley,*
> *Whose neighbours were mundane but mannerly.*
> *They don't cavil the least*
> *At a stray anapæst,*
> *But they do bar his spondees in Anerley.*

'I'll post this and send off my bundle of MSS. from
'Frisco.'

He left Tahiti in April. 'Last night,' he wrote on the
steamer, 'I looked for the Southern Cross as usual, and
looked for it in vain—like the moon for Omar Khay-
yam—it had gone down below the horizon. It is still
shining and wheeling for those good brown people
in the islands and they're laughing and kissing and
swimming and dancing beneath it—but for me it is
set; and I don't know that I shall ever see it again. It's
queer. I was sad at heart to leave Tahiti. But I resigned
myself to the vessel, and watched the green shores and
rocky peaks fade with hardly a pang. I had told so

many of those that loved me, so often, "oh, yes, I'll come back—next year perhaps, or the year after"— that I suppose I'd begun to believe it myself. It was only yesterday, when I knew that the Southern Cross had left me, that I suddenly realised I had left behind those lovely places and lovely people, perhaps for ever. I reflected that there was surely nothing else like them in this world, and very probably nothing in the next, and that I was going far away from gentleness and beauty and kindliness, and the smell of the lagoons, and the thrill of that dancing, and the scarlet of the flamboyants, and the white and gold of other flowers; and that I was going to America, which is full of harshness and hideous sights, and ugly people, and civilisation, and corruption, and bloodiness, and all evil. So I wept a little, and very sensibly went to bed. . . . . . .

'Certain reprehensible corners of my heart whisper to me, "There's a village in Samoa, with the moonlight on the beach"—or "I've heard of a hill in Japan" —or "one said there's an inn in Thibet over a sheer precipice"—or "the Victoria Nyanza is an attractive lake"—or "that trail in the North-West up the Mackenzie—Morris said he'd go whenever I wanted"— —or "I wonder if it's true about that flower in the Andes that smells like no other flower upon earth, and when once a man has smelt it he can't but return there to live in those hills in the end, though he come back from the ends of the earth.". . . . . .

'I'll be Wordsworth's lark, that soars but doesn't roam, true to the kindred points of heaven and home.

These scraps of English poetry start whispering within me—that means I'm North of the Equator, doesn't it? It's a good sign, perhaps. English thoughts are waking in me. They'll fetch me back. Call me home, I pray you. I've been away long enough. I'm older than I was. I've left bits of me about—some of my hair in Canada, and one skin in Honolulu, and another in Fiji, and a bit of a third in Tahiti, and half a tooth in Samoa, and bits of my heart all over the place. I'm deader than I was. *Partir, c'est toujours mourir un peu*— you know that admirable and true proverb, don't you? A little old Frenchman, a friend of mine, told it me as we leaned over the rail and watched the waving crowds and the red roofs and the hills and the clouds dwindle and vanish. He was going home to France for a year for his health. "Home," he'd be angry at that. "*Mon* home *c'est ici*," he told me repeatedly. He is married to a native woman these fifteen years—no children of his own, but plenty adopted. She was so much finer than a white woman, he sighed—so lovely, so faithful, so competent, so charming and happy, and so extraordinarily intelligent. I told him what Tagore told me about white women compared with Indian, and he gave me his observations, and we entirely agreed, and forgot our sorrows in inventing bilingual insults to the swarms of ugly American and Colonial girls on board.'

'Oh, God! Oh, God!' his next letter to me began, from San Francisco in April. 'How I hate civilisation and houses and trams and collars.' But the shock was tempered to him. 'I've found good friends in the quieter parts of this region, who live in a garden filled with roses and hyacinths and morning-glory. So I'll rest a day or two and try to get over the effects of my first re-entry into civilisation. And then I'll sneak away East and come home. I want to live in a hut by a river and pretend I'm Polynesian. Will you come and see me o' week-ends?....... Oh! Oh! I am old as death. *Urana!*' And from the train: 'I read books on *Indirect Primaries*,[1] just to get the South Seas out of my blood. One must remember one has trousers on again. I had a faint thought of going to Mexico. But I guess it won't be much of a war. You'll be vanishing for Whitsuntide soon. A yachting trip to Ulster? I do hope you're going to let the Orangemen slit all the priests' throats first; and then shoot *them*. I'll enlist on either side, any day: Your nostic,

RUPERT.'

'It's eleven months,' he wrote to Miss Nesbitt from Arizona, 'that I've not been looked after, and my clothes are in an awful state, and my hair not cut, and I rarely shave. I'm so tired of it. Comprenny? Do you get me? I shall—(prepare your ears and hold tight)— shall sail from New York on June 6th and by June 15th I shall be in London. My dear, one thing I would implore you. It's very silly. But don't tell anybody the exact day I'm coming back. It's my fancy to blow in on them unexpected—just to wander into Ray-

---

[1] He was also reading Boswell. 'I've discovered,' he wrote, 'that Dr Johnson is the only man I love. An Englishman, by God!'

mond Buildings and hear Eddie squeak "Oh, *my dear*, I thought you were in Tahiti!" It's *awfly* silly and romantic, but the thought does give me the keenest and most exquisite pleasure. Don't give away one of the first poets in England—but there is in him still a very very small portion that's just a little childish.'

'I have such news,' he wrote in his next letter. 'It begins with Maurice Browne[1] and his wife going to Europe a week sooner than I had planned to. We squabbled, I saying they should defer their departure a week for the pleasure of going with me; they, ridiculously, that I should hasten my leaving this land some seven days for the honour of their companionship. Neither side would yield; so we parted in wrath. They pettily, I with some dignity. Coming here, I found two engagements fallen through; and last night I dreamed very vividly that I arrived in England, and telephoned to everybody I knew, and they were *awfully* nice, and then went round and saw them and they were *lovely*. Friends I had known long ago, between whom and myself evil and pain has come, greeted me in the old first way; and other friends who have stayed friends were wonderfully the same; and there were new friends. . . . . . . I woke laughing and crying. I felt I *must* get back. I telephoned to Browne, flew to some agents, and in consequence I sail from New York on May 29th, and reach Plymouth—oh blessed name, oh loveliness! Plymouth—was there ever so sweet and droll a sound? Drake's Plymouth, English Western Plymouth, city where men speak

[1] Director of the Little Theatre at Chicago.

softly, and things are sold for shillings, not for dollars; and there is love, and beauty, and old houses; and beyond which there are little fields, very green, bounded by small piled walls of stone; and behind them—I know it—the brown and black, splintered, haunted moor. By that the train shall go up; by Dartmouth, where my brother was—I will make a litany; by Torquay, where Verrall stayed; and by Paignton, where I have walked in the rain; past Ilsington, where John Ford was born, and Appledore, in the inn of which I wrote a poem against a commercial traveller; by Dawlish, of which John Keats sang; within sight of Widdicombe, where old Uncle Tom Cobley rode a mare; not a dozen miles from John Galsworthy at Manaton; within sight almost of that hill at Drewsteignton on which I lay out all one September night, crying—and to Exeter, and to Ottery St Mary where Coleridge sojourned; and across Wiltshire, where men built and sang many centuries before the Aquila. Oh noble train, oh glorious and forthright and English train! I will look round me at the English faces, and out at the English fields, and I will pray——reach Plymouth, as I was saying when I was interrupted, on Friday, June 5th.'

I got wind of his design to arrive like a bolt from the blue, and represented the disaster it would be if he came and found the door closed against him. He yielded, and at 2.45 a.m. on June 6th (for the forthright English train was very late) Denis Browne and I met him at Paddington.

VI

ALL the old threads were picked up at once. 'To the poor stay-at-home,' writes Walter de la Mare, 'the friend who placidly reappeared from the ends of the earth seemed as little changed as one who gaily and laughingly goes to bed and gaily and laughingly comes down next morning after a perfectly refeshing sleep.' He was still exactly the 'Young Apollo' of Mrs Cornford's Cambridge epigram; though the glint of quite peculiarly real shining gold that had always been in his hair had been tanned out of it by the Southern sun; and though one felt, in a hundred indefinable ways, that he was now more than ever 'prepared'; not, as it turned out, for the 'long littleness of life,' but rather for its brief greatness.

The morning after his return he hurried off to Rugby for a few days with his Mother. Then he had six crowded, happy weeks, mostly in London, seeing old friends and making new ones—including Lascelles Abercrombie, whom he met for the first time, though they had long been friends by proxy and by correspondence. His shyness, which had always been a part of his rather curious modesty and 'unspoiltness,' was wearing off; and I am told he confessed, on being asked, that it had now dawned upon him for the first time that when he came into a room where there were new people the chances were that they would like him, rather than not.

At the end of July came the war-cloud—and then the war. He has described his feelings when he heard the news in the essay *An Unusual Young Man* (the setting is imaginary—he was not returning from a cruise, but staying with the Cornfords in Norfolk). At first he was just unhappy and bewildered. 'I'm so uneasy—subconsciously,' he wrote. 'All the vague perils of the time—the world seems so dark—and I'm vaguely frightened. I feel hurt to think that France may suffer. And it hurts, too, to think that Germany may be harmed by Russia. And I'm anxious that England may act rightly. I can't *bear* it if she does wrong.'

'I've just been to a music-hall,' he wrote early in August. 'It was pretty full. Miss C. Loftus was imitating somebody I saw infinite years ago—Elsie Janis— in her imitation of a prehistoric figure called Frank Tinney. God! how far away it all seemed. Then a dreadful cinematographic reproduction of a hand drawing patriotic things—Harry Furniss it was, funny pictures of a soldier and a sailor (at the time I suppose dying in Belgium), a caricature of the Kaiser, greeted with a perfunctory hiss—nearly everyone sat silent. Then a scribbled message was shown: "War declared with Austria 11.9." There was a volley of quick, low hand-clapping—more a signal of recognition than anything else. Then we dispersed into Trafalgar Square and bought midnight War editions. . . . In all these days I haven't been so near tears; there was such tragedy and dignity in the people. . . . . . .

'If there's any good in anything I've done, it's made

by the beauty and goodness of . . . a few I've known. All these people at the front who are fighting muddledly enough for some idea called England—it's some faint shadowing of goodness and loveliness they have in their hearts to die for.'

For the first day or two he did not realise that he must fight—one of his ideas was to go to France and help get in the crops. But before we had been at war a week he was back in London, seeking out the best way to serve as a soldier. 'I've spent a fortnight,' he wrote on August 24th, 'in chasing elusive employment about. For a time I got drilled on the chance of getting into a London corps as a private, but now I really think I shall get a commission, Territorial probably, through Cambridge. The whole thing, and the insupportable stress of this time, tired me to a useless rag.'

Early in September Winston Churchill offered him a commission in the Royal Naval Division, then forming; and he and Denis Browne[1] joined the Anson

---

[1] I may here briefly commemorate William Denis Browne, whose death at 26 left no monument of his powers, except a few songs of great beauty. He was a musician of rare promise and complete equipment; and I have high authority for saying that his grasp of the foundations and tendencies of modern music was unique. I cannot here describe the singular charm of his character and personality. Enough that he never failed in honour, or in kindness, or in good sense, or in humour; and there were many who loved him.

He was a friend of Rupert's at Rugby, at Cambridge, and in London; last, his brother-in-arms; and he cared for him, as will be told, in his mortal illness. Six weeks afterwards, on the

Battalion on September 27th. I saw them off to Betteshanger Camp from Charing Cross—excited and a little shy, like two new boys going to school—happy and handsome in their new uniforms, and specially proud of their caps, which had very superior badges.

The Anson soon went to Chatham for musketry, and there he wrote: 'Often enough I feel a passing despair. I mean what you meant—the gulf between non-combatants and combatants. Yet it's not that—it's the withdrawal of combatants into a special seclusion and reserve. We're under a curse—or a blessing, or a vow to be different. The currents of our lives are interrupted. What is it? . . . I know—yes. The central purpose of my life, the aim and end of it now, the thing God wants of me, is to get good at beating Germans. That's sure. But that isn't what it *was*. What it was, I never knew; and God knows I never found it. But it reached out deeply for other things than my present need. . . . There *is* the absence. Priests and criminals—we're both—are celibates . . . and so I feel from my end sometimes that it *is* a long, long way to Tipperary. And yet, all's well. I'm the happiest person in the world.'

There were humours in the life; for instance, a false alarm of invasion at Chatham, when 'elderly men rushed about pulling down swords from the mess-room walls, and fastened them on with safety-pins'; or this incident in the day's routine: 'I had to make an

4th of June, he followed him, fighting with high gallantry in the attack on the Turkish trenches before Krithia.

inventory the other day of all their kit, to compare with what they *should* have. I soon found that questions about some of the articles on the lists were purely academic. "How many handkerchiefs have you?" The first two men were prompted to say "none." The third was called Cassidy. "How many phwat, sorr?" "Handkerchiefs." — "?" — "Handkerchiefs, man, handkerchiefs." (*In a hoarse whisper to the Petty Officer*) "Phwat does he mane?" P.O. (*in a stage whisper*), "Ter blow yer nose with, yer bloody fool." Cassidy (*rather indignant*), "None, sorr!" They were dears, and very strong, some of them.'

On the 4th of October they sailed for Antwerp. When it was all over, and he was having a little leave in London, he wrote to a friend: 'I've been extremely slack and sleepy these last few days. I think it was the reaction after the excitement. Also I caught *conjunctivitis*, alias pink-eye, in some of the foul places we slept in; and my eyes have been swollen, red, unlovely, exuding a thick plum-tree gum, and very painful. I *hope* they're getting better. . . . . . . It's only a fortnight ago! We were pulled out of bed at 5 a.m. on the Sunday, and told that we started at 9. We marched to Dover, highly excited, only knowing that we were bound for Dunkirk, and supposing that we'd stay there quietly, training, for a month. Old ladies waved handkerchiefs, young ladies gave us apples, and old men and children cheered, and we cheered back, and I felt very elderly and sombre, and full of thought of how human life was a flash between darkness, and that *x* per cent. of those who cheered would be blown into another world within a few months; and they all seemed to me so innocent and pathetic and noble, and my eyes grew round and tear-stained....... [Arrived at Dunkirk] we sat in a great empty shed a quarter of a mile long, waiting for orders. After dark the senior officers rushed round and informed us that we were going to Antwerp, that our train was sure to be attacked, and that if we got through we'd have to sit in trenches till we were wiped out. So we all sat under lights writing last letters, a very tragic and amusing affair. It *did* bring home to me how very futile and unfinished my life was. I felt so angry. I had to imagine, supposing I *was* killed. There was nothing except a vague gesture of good-bye to you and my mother and a friend or two. I seemed so remote and barren and stupid. I seemed to have missed everything.

'We *weren't* attacked that night in the train. So we got out at Antwerp and marched through the streets, and everyone cheered and flung themselves on us, and gave us apples and chocolate and flags and kisses, and cried *Vivent les Anglais* and "Heep! Heep! Heep!"

'We got out to a place called Vieux Dieux (or something like it), passing refugees and Belgian soldiers by millions. Every mile the noises got louder, immense explosions and detonations. We stopped in the town square at Vieux Dieux; five or six thousand British troops, a lot of Belgians, guns going through, transport-waggons, motor-cyclists, orderlies on horses, staff officers, and the rest. An extraordinary and thrilling confusion. As it grew dark the thunders increased, and the sky was lit by extraordinary glares. We were all given entrenching tools. Everybody looked worried. Suddenly our battalion was marched round the corner out of the din, through an old gate in the immense wild garden of a recently deserted villa-château. There we had to sleep. On the rather dirty and wild-looking sailors trudged, over lawns, through orchards, and across pleasaunces. Little pools glimmered through the trees, and deserted fountains; and round corners one saw, faintly, occasional Cupids and Venuses—a scattered company of rather bad statues—gleaming quietly. The sailors dug their latrines in the various rose-gardens, and lay down to sleep—but it was bitter cold—under the shrubs. By two the shells had got unpleasantly near, and some message came. So up we got—frozen and sleepy—and toiled off through the night. By dawn we got into trenches—very good ones—and relieved Belgians.

'This is *very* dull. And it doesn't really reflect my state of mind. For when I think back on it, my mind is filled with various disconnected images and feelings. And if I could tell you these fully, you *might* find it wonderful, or at least queer. There's the excitement in the trenches (we weren't attacked seriously in our part) with people losing their heads and fussing and snapping. It's queer to see the people who *do* break under the strain of danger and responsibility. It's always the rotten ones. Highly sensitive people don't, queerly enough. I was relieved to find I was incredibly brave! I don't know how I should behave if shrapnel were bursting over me and knocking the men round me to pieces. But for risks and nerves and fatigues I was all right. That's cheering.

'And there's the empty blue sky and the peaceful village and country scenery, and nothing of war to see except occasional bursts of white smoke, very lazy and quiet, in the distance. But to hear—incessant thunder, shaking buildings and ground, and you and everything; and above, recurrent wailings, very thin and queer, like lost souls, crossing and recrossing in the emptiness—nothing to be seen. Once or twice a lovely glittering aeroplane, very high up, would go over us; and then the shrapnel would be turned on it, and a dozen quiet little curls of white smoke would appear round the creature—the whole thing like a German woodcut, very quaint and peaceful and unreal.

'But the retreat drowned all these impressions. We stole away from the trenches, across half Antwerp, over the Scheldt, and finally entrained in the last train left, at 7.30 next morning. The march through those deserted suburbs, mile on mile, with never a living being, except our rather ferocious-looking sailors stealing sulkily along. The sky was lit by burning villages and houses; and after a bit we got to the land by the river, where the Belgians had let all the petrol out of the tanks and fired it. Rivers and seas of flames leaping up hundreds of feet, crowned by black smoke that covered the entire heavens. It lit up houses wrecked by shells, dead horses, demolished railway-stations, engines that had been taken up with their lines and signals, and all twisted round and pulled out, as a bad child spoils a toy. . . . . . . The glare was like hell. We passed on, out of that, across a pontoon bridge built on boats. Two German spies tried to blow it up while we were on it. They were caught and shot. We went on through the dark. The refugees and motor-buses and transport and Belgian troops grew thicker. After about a thousand years it was dawn. The motor-buses indicated that we were bound for Hammersmith, and might be allowed to see *Potash and Perlmutter.*'

Another letter, written on Christmas Day to Russell Loines of New York, perhaps his greatest friend among his kind American hosts, shows how deeply the sight of the refugees had moved him. 'I started a long letter to you in August and September, in my scraps of time; a valuable letter, full of information about the war and the state of mind of pacifists and others. The Germans have it now. It went in my luggage to Antwerp, and there was left. Whether it was burnt or captured, I can't be sure. But it was in a tin box, with—damn it!—a lot of my manuscript. And it was fairly heavily shelled.

'I don't know if you heard of my trip to Antwerp. A queer picnic. They say we saved the Belgian army, and most of the valuable things in the town—stores and ammunition, I mean. With luck, we might have kept the line fifty miles forward of where it is. However, we at last got away—most of us. It really was a very mild experience; except the thirty miles march out through the night and the blazing city. Antwerp that night was like several different kinds of hell—the broken houses and dead horses lit up by an infernal glare. The refugees were the worst sight. The German policy of frightfulness had succeeded so well, that out of that city of half a million, when it was decided to surrender Antwerp, not ten thousand would stay. They put their goods on carts, barrows, perambulators, anything. Often the carts had no horses, and they just stayed there in the street, waiting for a miracle There were all the country refugees, too, from the villages, who had been coming through our lines all day and half the night. I'll never forget that white-faced, endless procession in the night, pressed aside to let the military—us—pass, crawling forward at some hundred yards an hour, quite hopeless, the old men crying, and the women with hard drawn faces. What a crime!—and I gather they've announced their intention of *keeping* Belgium if they can.

'England is remarkable. I wish I had the time to describe it. But this job keeps one so darned tired, and so stupid, that I haven't the words. There are a few people who've been so anti-war before, or so suspicious of diplomacy, that they feel rather out of the national feeling. But it's astonishing to see how the "intellectuals" have taken on new jobs. No, not astonishing; but impressive. Masefield drills hard in Hampstead, and told me, with some pride, a month ago, that he was a Corporal, and *thought* he was going to be promoted to Sergeant soon. Cornford is no longer the best Greek scholar in Cambridge. He recalled that he was a very good shot in his youth, and is now a Sergeant-Instructor of Musketry. I'm here.

My brother is a 2nd Lieutenant in the Post Office
Rifles. He was one of three great friends at King's.
The second is Intelligence Officer in H.M.S. *Ven-
geance*, Channel Patrol. The third is buried near Cam-
brai. Gilbert Murray and Walter Raleigh rise at six
every day to line hedgerows in the dark, and "ad-
vance in rushes" across the Oxford meadows.

'Among the other officers in this Division whom I
know are two young Asquiths;[1] an Australian pro-
fessional pianist[2] who twice won the Diamond Sculls;
a New Zealander[3] who was fighting in Mexico and
walked 300 miles to the coast to get a boat when he
heard of the War; a friend of mine, Denis Browne—
Cambridge—who is one of the best young English
musicians and an extremely brilliant critic; a youth
lately through Eton and Balliol,[4] who is the most
brilliant man they've had in Oxford for ten years; a
young and very charming American called John
Bigelow Dodge, who turned up to "fight for the
right"—I could extend the list. It's all a terrible tragedy. And yet, in its details, it's great fun. And—
apart from the tragedy—I've never felt happier or
better in my life than in those days in Belgium. And
now I've the feeling of anger at a seen wrong—Belgium—to make me happier and more resolved in my

[1] Brigadier-General Arthur Asquith, D.S.O., and his brother
Herbert.
[2] F. S. Kelly, killed in action.
[3] Now Major-General Sir Bernard Freyberg, K.C.B., V.C.,
D.S.O.
[4] Patrick Shaw-Stewart, killed in action.

work. I know that whatever happens, I'll be doing some good, fighting to prevent *that*.'

'I hope to get through,' he wrote about the same time to Mrs Arnold Toynbee. 'I'll have such a lot to say and do afterwards. Just now I'm rather miserable, because most of my school-friends are wounded, or "wounded and missing," or dead. Perhaps our sons will live the better for it all. I knew of yours, I was very glad. It must be good to have a son. When they told us at Dunkirk that we were all going to be killed in Antwerp, if not on the way there, I didn't think much (as I'd expected) what a damned fool I was not to have written more, and done various things better, and been less selfish. I merely thought "what *Hell* it is that I shan't have any children—any sons." I thought it over and over, quite furious, for some hours. And we were barely even under fire, in the end!'

'There's a lot to talk about,' he told Jacques Raverat 'though I'm rather beyond talking. Yes, we *are* insular. Did you hear of the British private who had been through the fighting from Mons to Ypres, and was asked what he thought of all his experiences? He said, "What I don't like about this 'ere b—— Europe is all these b—— pictures of Jesus Christ and His relations, behind b—— bits of glawss."[1] It seems to me to express perfectly that insularity and cheerful atheism which are the chief characteristics of my race.

'All the same, though myself cheerful, insular, and an atheist, I'm largely dissatisfied with the English,

[1] This was a story of Julian Grenfell's about one of his men, which I had passed on to Rupert.

just now. The good ones are all right. And it's curiously far away from us (if we haven't the Belgians in memory as I have). But there's a ghastly sort of apathy over half the country. And I really think large numbers of male people don't want to die. Which is odd. I've been praying for a German raid. . . . . . .

'My mind's gone stupid with drill and arranging about the men's food. It's all good fun. I'm rather happy. I've a restful feeling that all's going well and I'm not harming anyone, and probably even doing good. A queer new feeling. The only horror is that I want to marry in a hurry and get a child, before I vanish. . . . . . . There's the question: to ponder in my sleeping-bag, between the thoughts on the attack and calculations about the boots of the platoon. Insoluble: and the weeks slip on. It'll end in my muddling that, as I've muddled everything else.'

After they got back from Antwerp, there was a tiresome period of re-shuffling among the different battalions; but by the middle of December, Rupert, Denis Browne, Arthur Asquith, Patrick Shaw-Stewart, Bernard Freyberg, and the rest were re-united at Blandford Camp in the 'Hood,' where there were other officers who were either friends already or belonged to conterminous sets; so that a pleasant family party was soon established. The life was strenuous, but not eventful. 'I spend Christmas,'[1] he wrote, 'in looking after drunken stokers. One of them has been drunk since 7 a.m.; he neither eats nor drinks,

[1] He had telegraphed just before, to a trusty friend, 'Send mince-pies for sixty men and a few cakes immediately.'

hut dances a complicated step up and down his hut, singing, "How happy I am, how happy I am"—a short, fat, inelegant man, in stockinged feet. What wonders we are! There's no news—occasional scares. On Wednesday I (don't tell a soul) started a sonnet. What a fall!'

The five sonnets called '1914' had been coming for some time, and were finished at Rugby when he went there for a few days' leave just after Christmas. 'These proofs have come,' he wrote from Canford Manor on January 24th. 'My muse, panting all autumn under halberd and cuirass, could but falter these syllables through her vizor. God, they're in the rough, these five camp-children—4 and 5 are good enough, and there are phrases in the rest.[1]

'Last night I slept between sheets, and this morning I lay an hour in a hot bath, and so was late for a breakfast of pheasant and sausages and the divinest coffee. Now I sit over a great fire of wood in the hall of a house built by Vanbrugh, with a Scuola di Bellini above me, smoking and reading and writing.

'I've been peacefully reading up the countryside all the morning. Where our huts are was an Iberian fort against the Celts—and Celtish against Romans—and Roman against Saxons. . . . Just over the hills is that tower where a young Astronomer watched the stars,

---

[1] 'I think *reading* in war-time right enough,' he wrote to Miss Pye from the Mediterranean. 'But writing requires a longer period of serenity, a more certainly undisturbed subconsciousness. If the S.C.'s turbulent, one's draught from it is opaque. Witness the first three sonnets.'

and a Lady watched the Astronomer.[1] By Tarrant Hinton, two miles North, George Bubb Dodington lived and reigned and had his salon. In Tarrant Crawford, two miles South, a Queen lies buried. Last week we attacked some of the New Army in Badbury Rings—an ancient fort where Arthur defeated the Saxons in—what year? Where I lay on my belly cursing the stokers for their slowness, Guinevere sat, and wondered if she'd see Arthur or Lancelot return from the fight, or both, or neither, and pictured how they'd look; and then fell a-wondering which, if it came to the point, she'd prefer to see.'

'The world's going well,' he wrote at this time to Jacques Raverat: 'better than it did when we were younger. And a Frenchman is the one person in the world with something to be proud of, these days.'

VII

ON January 29th he came to London to recover from a rather bad attack of influenza, staying first at Gray's Inn and then at 10 Downing Street. I saw him for the last time on February 25th, when the King reviewed the Naval Division at Blandford before their departure for the Dardanelles. The secret of where they were going was just out, and everyone was wild with excitement and joy. 'It's too wonderful for belief,' he wrote to Miss Asquith. 'I had not imagined Fate could be so benign. I almost suspect her. Perhaps we shall be held in reserve, out of sight, on a

[1] See Thomas Hardy's *Two on a Tower.*

choppy sea, for two months. . . . Yet even that! . . .
But I'm filled with confident and glorious hopes. I've
been looking at the maps. Do you think *perhaps* the
fort on the Asiatic corner will want quelling, and
we'll land and come at it from behind, and they'll
make a sortie and meet us on the plains of Troy? It
seems to me strategically so possible. Shall we have a
Hospital Base (and won't you manage it?) on Lesbos?
Will Hero's Tower crumble under the 15″ guns?
Will the sea be polyphloisbic and wine-dark and
unvintageable? Shall I loot mosaics from St Sophia,
and Turkish Delight, and carpets? Should we be a
Turning Point in History? Oh God!

'I've never been quite so happy in my life, I think.
Not quite so pervasively happy; like a stream flowing
entirely to one end. I suddenly realise that the ambition of my life has been—since I was two—to go on
a military expedition against Constantinople. And
when I *thought* I was hungry or sleepy or aching to
write a poem—*that* was what I really, blindly, wanted. This is nonsense. Good-night. I'm very tired with
equipping my platoon.'

They sailed from Avonmouth in the *Grantully
Castle* on February 28th. 'Four days out,' he dated his
next letter to Miss Asquith. 'All day we've been just
out of sight of land, thirty or forty miles away—out
of sight, but in smell. There was something earthy in
the air, and warm—like the consciousness of a presence in the dark—the wind had something Anda-
lusian in it. It wasn't that wall of scent and invisible
blossom and essential spring that knocks you flat,

quite suddenly, as you've come round some unseen corner in the atmosphere, fifty miles out from a South Sea Island; but it *was* the good smell of land—and of Spain, too! And Spain I've never seen, and never shall see, may be. All day I sat and strained my eyes to see over the horizon orange-groves and Moorish buildings, and dark-eyed beauties, and guitars, and fountains, and a golden darkness. But the curve of the world lay between us. Do you know Jan [Masefield]'s favourite story—told very melodiously with deep-voice reverence—about Columbus? Columbus wrote a diary (which Jan reads) and described the coast of America as he found it—*the* divinest place in the world. "It was only like the Paradise of the Saints of God"—and then he remembered that there was *one* place equal to it, the place where he was born—and goes on "or like the gardens of Andalusia in the spring." '

He wrote to me from 'North of Tunis' on March 7th. 'It seems ages ago since we said good-bye to you on our mottled parade-ground. We've had rather a nice voyage; a bit unsteady the first day (when I was sick) and to-day; otherwise very smooth and delicious. There has been a little, not much, to do. I've read most of *Turkey in Europe*. But what with parades and the reading of military books, I've not written anything. Anyway, my mind's always a blank at sea.

'For two days we've been crawling along the African Coast, observing vast tawny mountains, with white villages on this side of them and white peaks beyond. The sea has been a jewel, and sunset and dawn divine blazes of colour. It's all too ridiculously peaceful for one to believe anything but that we're a —rather odd—lot of tourists, seeing the Mediterranean and bent on enjoyment. War seems infinitely remote; and even the reason, foreseeing Gallipoli, yet admits that there are many blue days to come, and the Cyclades. . . . . . .

'I can well see that life might be great fun; and I can well see death might be an admirable solution. . . . . . .

'In a fortnight, the quarter million Turks.'

I think these words on the prospect of living or dying represent his normal state of mind; and that he had nothing which could justly be called a *presentiment* of death. 'This is very odd,' was the beginning of a letter which he wrote for me in case he died. 'But I suppose I must imagine my non-existence, and make a few arrangements.' He certainly spoke to some people as though he were sure of not coming back; but no one can read the letters I have printed without seeing what a creature of moods he was; and it was always his way to dramatise the future. There was a vivid realisation of the possibility—I believe that was all.[1]

[1] The preoccupation with the idea of death, shown in his poems from the first, has been often noticed. When I looked through his copy of Aristophanes, I was struck by a heavy triple mark which he had put against two lines of the *Frogs*—almost the only passage he had marked at all:

τεθνηκόσιν γὰρ ἔλεγεν ὦ μοχθηρὲ σύ,
οἷς οὐδὲ τρὶς λέγοντες ἐξικνούμεθα.

'*Aye, but he's speaking to the dead, you knave,*
Who cannot hear us though we call them thrice.' (Rogers)

This may have suggested the phrase about the 'unanswering

He spoke in the letter I have just quoted of a wish he had expressed to his Mother (which she has carried out), that any money he left, and any profits from his books, should be divided between three of his brother poets. 'If I can set them free to any extent,' he told her, 'to write the poetry and plays and books they want to, my death will bring more gain than loss.' The three were Lascelles Abercrombie, Walter de la Mare, and Wilfrid Gibson.[1]

'We had a very amusing evening in Malta,' he wrote

dead' in *Ambarvalia*, which occurs again in a fragment, probably written in 1914:

> *'We have told you the last lies, unanswering Dead.*
> *Farewell, we have said;*
> *Knowing the Dead fare neither ill nor well.*

---

[1] Mrs Brooke included in this bequest the amount of the Howland Memorial Prize, the first award of which was unanimously made to her son in 1916, after his death, by the Committee of the Corporation of Yale University. The prize is given 'in recognition of some achievement of marked distinction in the field of literature or fine arts or the science of government; and an important factor in the selection is the idealistic element in the recipient's work.'

Mr Charles Howland wrote to Mrs Brooke announcing the award: 'You must have known already by many avenues of the feeling about him in the United States—of the sense of tenderness for his youth, of the attitude of possession of him jointly with Englishmen as one of the Masters of Song in our common tongue; and indeed that he typifies the nobility of sacrifice for a cause that is ours as well as yours.'

The lecture, which by the terms of the gift was due from the prizewinner, was delivered at Yale by Walter de la Mare in his stead.

to his Mother on March 12th. 'Our boat got in one afternoon almost last of the lot. We were allowed ashore from 5 to midnight. Oc,[1] Denis, and I drove round in a funny little carriage, and looked at the views. It's a very lovely place; very like Verona or any Italian town, but rather cleaner and more Southern. There was a lovely Mediterranean sunset and evening, and the sky and sea were filled with colours. The odd and pleasant thing was the way we kept running into people we knew and hadn't expected to meet. First there were people in all the other battalions, who had come on by other boats. Then we found "Cardy" [Lionel] Montagu, E.S.M.'s brother, staring at the Cathedral. Then Cherry, who used to be in the Anson with us, a nice chap, and he dined with us; and in, at the end of dinner, came Patrick Shaw-Stewart (of this Battalion) with Charles Lister, who was dragged in absolutely at the last moment because he is supposed to know Turkish, and is with the Divisional Staff. Before dinner, as I was buying buttons in a little shop, in walked George Peel! And after dinner, at a nice little opera, everyone I knew seemed to appear, in khaki, all very cheerful and gay. Lots of people who we thought were going to be left behind had been able to get out at the last moment, and pounced on us from behind boxes or out of stalls. The Maltese *élite* who were there must have been puzzled at the noise.'

From Malta they went on to Lemnos; 'the *loveliest* place in the evening sun,' he wrote, 'softly white,

[1] Arthur Asquith.

grey, silver-white buildings, some very old, some new, round a great harbour—all very Southern; like an Italian town in silver-point, livable and serene, with a sea and sky of opal and pearl and faint gold around. It was nearer than any place I've ever seen to what a Greek must have witnessed when he sailed into a Greek coast-city.'

Here there was an alarum, but not an excursion, as appears from a letter to Miss Cox, dated 'Somewhere (some way from the front) March 19th.' 'The other day we—some of us—were told that we sailed next day to make a landing. A few thousand of us. Off we stole that night through the phosphorescent Aegean, scribbling farewell letters, and snatching periods of excited dream-broken sleep. At four we rose, buckled on our panoply, hung ourselves with glasses, compasses, periscopes, revolvers, food, and the rest, and had a stealthy large breakfast. *That* was a mistake. It's ruinous to load up one's belly four or five hours before it expects it—it throws the machinery out of gear for a week. I felt extremely ill the rest of that day.

'We paraded in silence under paling stars along the sides of the ship. The darkness on the sea was full of scattered flashing lights, hinting at our fellow-transports and the rest. Slowly, the sky became warm and green, and the sea opal. Everyone's face looked drawn and ghastly. If we landed, my company was to be the first to land. . . . We made out that we were only a mile or two from a dim shore. I was seized with an agony of remorse that I hadn't taught my platoon a

155

thousand things more energetically and competently. The light grew. The shore looked to be crammed with Fate and was ominously silent. One man thought he saw a camel through his glasses. . . .

'There were some hours of silence.

'About seven, someone said, "We're going home." We dismissed the stokers, who said, quietly, "When's the next battle?" and disempanoplied, and had another breakfast. If we were a "feint," or if it was too rough to land, or in general, what little part we blindly played, we never knew, and shall not. Still, we did our bit, not ignobly, I trust. We did not see the enemy. We did not fire at them; nor they at us. It seemed improbable they saw us. One of B Company—she was rolling very slightly—was sick on parade. Otherwise, no casualties. A notable battle.

'Later. We're off to Egypt: for repose. For—I imagine—a month at least. What a life! Another campaign over!'

On March 27th they arrived at Port Said, and he went for three days' leave with Arthur Asquith and Patrick Shaw-Stewart to Cairo, where they saw the Sphinx and the Pyramids, rode about on camels, and bought things in the bazaars.

Sir Ian Hamilton came to Port Said to review the Naval Division on April 3rd, and offered him a post on his staff. 'I saw Rupert Brooke,' he wrote to me, 'lying down under a shelter, rather off colour, poor boy. He had got a touch of the sun the previous day. It was nothing, and essentially he was looking in first-class physical condition. He very naturally would like to see this first adventure through with his own men; after that I think he would like to come to me. It was very natural, and I quite understand it—I should have answered the same in his case had I been offered a staff billet.' Rupert never mentioned this offer to his brother-officers. 'The first day I was sick,' he wrote to his Mother, 'before I got out of camp—was the day when our new G.O.C.-in-Chief—you'll know who that is—reviewed us. I'd met him once or twice in London. He came to see me after the review and talked for a bit. He offered me a sort of galloper-aide-de-camp job on his staff: but I shan't take it. Anyhow, not now, not till this present job's over; afterwards, if I've had enough of the regimental officer's work, I might like it.' 'But it's really so jolly,' he wrote to me on the same occasion, 'being with Oc and Denis and Charles [Lister] and Patrick and Kelly, that it'd have to be very tempting company to persuade me to give it up.'

That evening he joined Patrick Shaw-Stewart, who had the same illness, at the Casino Hotel. 'Then began nearly a week of comic alternations and vicissitudes in our humiliating complaint,' Shaw-Stewart wrote to me. 'The companionship in our two little beds was very close, but limited by our mental state, which owing to starvation was—for me—complete vacuity. So we just lay opposite and grew our little beards, mine red, his golden brown, and made our little jokes at one another—very good ones, I can't help thinking. Altogether, if it hadn't been for the starvation and the uncomfortable beds and the terrible difficulty of making the Italian waiter understand (R. did better with gesticulatory English than I with Italian, which made me furious) it was the best period of the war for me. We were turned out rather quickly. On the Friday morning, April 9th, we were ordered to be aboard that evening if we were well enough, which of course we both said we were. In my case there was no doubt I was: in R.'s I think it was doubtful, and Colonel Quilter rather urged him to stay behind if he still felt queer, but of course it would have been a difficult thing (morally) to do. So we both went on board and stuck to our cabins for a day or two, R. emerging later than me. Just at this time he seemed really pretty well (as well as at Blandford, which I think for him probably wasn't so very well) but a little listless.'

Rupert himself wrote to Miss Asquith the day he left the hotel, 'Anyhow here I am, well up on that difficult slope that leads from arrowroot, past chicken broth, by rice puddings, to eggs in milk, and so to eggs, and boiled fish, and finally (they say) chicken and fruit and even real meat. But that is still beyond the next crest. On! on! But while I shall be well, I think, for our first thrust into the fray, I shall be able to give my Turk, at the utmost, a kitten's tap. A diet of arrowroot doesn't build up violence. I am as weak as a pacifist.'

About the same time he wrote to Lascelles Abercrombie: 'The Sun-God (he, the Song-God) distinguished one of his most dangerous rivals since Marsyas among the x thousand tanned and dirty men

blown suddenly on these his special coasts a few days
or weeks ago. He unslung his bow. . . . I lie in an
hotel, cool at length, with wet clothes on my head
and less than nothing in my belly. Sunstroke is a
bloody affair. It breaks very suddenly the fair harmonies of the body and the soul. I'm lying recovering
from it, living faintly on arrowroot and rice-puddings
and milk; passing from dream to dream, all faint and
tasteless and pure as arrowroot itself. I shall be all right
in time for the fighting, I hope and believe.

   '*Later* (*at sea*). I know now what a campaign is. I
had a suspicion from Antwerp. It is continual crossing
from one place to another, and back, over dreamlike
seas: anchoring, or halting, in the oddest places, for
no one knows or quite cares how long: drifting on,
at last, to some other equally unexpected, equally out
of the way, equally odd spot: for all the world like a
bottle in some corner of the bay at a seaside resort.
Somewhere, sometimes, there is fighting. Not for us.
In the end, no doubt, our apparently aimless course
will drift us through, or anchor us in, a blaze of
war, quite suddenly; and as suddenly swirl us out
again. Meanwhile, the laziest loitering lotus-day I idled
away as a wanderer in the South Seas was a bustle of
decision and purpose compared to a campaign.

   'One just hasn't, though, the time and detachment
to write, I find. But I've been collecting a few words,
detaching lines from the ambient air, collaring one
or two of the golden phrases that a certain wind blows
from (will the Censor let me say?) Olympus, across
these purple seas.'

VIII

Of the 'golden phrases,' only the merest fragments remain. He must have made up more in his head than he wrote down, for his last letter to me implies a good deal more than there is. 'The first few days afloat I was still convalescent. So I could lie in my bunk and read and write in a delicious solitude all day. I actually *did* jot down a line or two. Nothing yet complete (except a song, worthless alone, for Denis to put lovely notes around); but a sonnet or two almost done; and the very respectable and shapely skeleton of an ode-threnody. All of which shall travel to you if and when they are done. . . . . . . I must go and censor my platoon's letters. My long poem is to be about the existence—and non-locality—of England. And it contains the line—"In Avons of the heart her rivers run." Lovely, isn't it?'

There is only a small black note-book, from which I will put together what I can. There will be found in the appendix the little song called *The Dance*, mentioned in the letter, and a fragment which is almost his only attempt at blank verse—though even there rhyme steals in towards the end. Here are the scraps which seem to belong to the 'ode-threnody' on England:

> *All things are written in the mind.*
> *There the sure hills have station; and the wind*
> *Blows   in that placeless air.*
> *And there the white and golden birds go flying;*
> *And the stars wheel and shine; and woods are fair;*

FRAGMENTS

The light upon the snow is there,
                    and in that nowhere move
The trees and   ¹ and waters that we love.

And she for whom we die, she the undying
Mother of men
England!
       *   *   *

In Avons of the heart her rivers run.
       *   *   *

She is with all we have loved and found and known,
Closed in the little nowhere of the brain.
Only, of all our dreams,
Not the poor heap of   dust and stone,
This local earth, set in terrestrial streams,
Not this man, giving all for gold,
Nor that who has found evil good, nor these
Blind millions, bought and sold . . .
       *   *   *

She is not here, or now—
She is here, and now, yet nowhere—
We gave her birth, who bore us—
Our wandering feet have sought, but never found
   her—
She is built a long way off—
She, though all men be traitors, not betrayed—
Whose soil is love, and her stars justice, she—

¹ The word 'hands' is written here, I think by mistake for
'hills.' Compare 'the trees and waters and the gills' in his early
poem, *The Charm*.

161

Gracious with flowers,
And robed   *and glorious in the sea.*[1]

     *   *   *

She was in his eyes, but he could not see her.
And he was England, but he knew her not.

There are fragments of other poems; two about the expedition:

They say Achilles in the darkness stirred,
And   *Hector, his old enemy,*
Moved the great shades that were his limbs. They heard
More than Olympian thunder on the sea.

     *   *   *

            Death and Sleep
   Bear many a young Sarpedon home.

And this, headed 'Queen Elizabeth':

   And Priam and his fifty sons
   Wake all amazed, and hear the guns,
     And shake for Troy again.

Then there is this:

   'When Nobby tried,' the stokers say,
    'To stop a shrapnel with his belly,
   He   *away,*
    He left a lump of bleeding jelly.'

---

[1] This last set of lines, or rather jottings, is not written as if they were meant to be consecutive.

FRAGMENTS

But he went out, did Nobby Clark,[1]
Upon the illimitable dark,
Out of the fields where soldiers stray,
  Beyond parades, beyond reveille.

This is for one of the sonnets:

The poor scrap of a song that some man tried
Down in the troop-decks forrard, brought again
The day you sang it first, on a hill-side,
With April in the wind and in the brain.
And the woods were gold; and youth was in our hands.

*   *   *

      Oh lovers parted,
Oh all you lonely over all the world,
You that look out at morning empty-hearted,
Or you, all night turning uncomforted

*   *   *

Would God, would God, you could be comforted.

*   *   *

      Eyes that weep,
And a long time for love; and, after, sleep.

There are lines of a poem about evening, in which
he recurs to the hares in the Grantchester cornfields:

  And daylight, like a dust, sinks through the air,
  And drifting, golds the ground . . .

[1] All sailors whose name is Clark are nicknamed Nobby. No
one knows why.

MEMOIR

A lark,
A voice in heaven, in fading deeps of light,
Drops, at length, home.

*   *   *

A wind of night, shy as the young hare
That steals even now out of the corn to play,
Stirs the pale river once, and creeps away.

And of an elegy:

The feet that ran with mine have found their goal,
The eyes that met my eyes have looked on night.
The firm limbs are no more; gone back to earth,
Easily mingling . . .
                      What he is yet,
Not living, lives, hath place in a few minds . . .
                                        He wears
The ungathered blossom of quiet; stiller he
Than a deep well at noon, or lovers met;
Than sleep, or the heart after wrath. He is
The silence following great words of peace.

That is all.

On the 17th of April they landed at Scyros. Arthur Asquith described it to his sister before anything had happened: 'This island is more mountainous than Lemnos, and more sparsely inhabited. It is like one great rock-garden of white and pinkish-white marble, with small red poppies and every sort of wildflower; in the gorges ilex, dwarf holly, and occasional groups of olives; and everywhere the smell of thyme (or is it sage? or wild mint?). Our men kill adders and have fun with big tortoises. The water near the shore, where the bottom is white marble, is more beautifully green and blue than I have ever seen it anywhere.'

Here then, in the island where Theseus was buried, and whence the young Achilles and the young Pyrrhus were called to Troy, Rupert Brooke died and was buried on Friday, the 23rd of April, the day of Shakespeare and of St George.

He seemed quite well till Tuesday the 20th, when there was a Divisional Field-day, and he went to bed tired immediately after dinner. On Wednesday he stayed in bed with pains in his back and head, and a swelling on his lip; but no anxiety was felt till the evening, when he had a temperature of 103. Next morning he was much worse; the swelling had increased, and a consultation was held. The diagnosis was acute blood-poisoning, and all hope was given up. It was decided to move him to the French hospital-ship *Duguay-Trouin* which happened to be at Scyros. When he was told this, his one anxiety was lest he should have difficulty in rejoining his battalion. They reassured him, and he seemed to be content. Soon afterwards he became comatose; and there does not seem to have been any moment when he can have realised that he was dying. The rest of the story shall be told in the words of the letter which Denis Browne wrote me on the 25th from the transport.

'In less than half an hour we had carried him down into a pinnace and taken him straight aboard the *Duguay-Trouin*. They put him in the best cabin, on the sun-deck. Everything was very roomy and comfortable; they had every modern appliance and the surgeons did all that they possibly could.[1] Oc and I left him about 6 when we could do nothing more, and went to the *Franconia*, where we sent a wireless message to the Admiralty.[2] Next morning Oc and I went over to see what we could do, and found him much weaker. There was nothing to be done, as he was quite unconscious and they were busy trying all the devices they could think of to give him ease. Not that he was suffering, for he was barely conscious all Thursday (he just said "Hallo" when I went to lift him out into the pinnace), and on Friday he was not conscious at all up to the very last, and felt no pain whatever. At 2 the head surgeon told me he was sinking. Oc went off to see about arrangements, and I sat with Rupert. At 4 o'clock he became weaker, and at 4.46 he died, with the sun shining all round his cabin, and the cool sea-breeze blowing through the door and the shaded windows. No one could have wished a quieter or a calmer end than in that lovely bay, shielded by the mountains and fragrant with sage and thyme.[3]

[1] 'I do want you to feel,' Browne wrote to Mrs Brooke, 'that nothing was left undone that could alleviate his condition, or prolong his life. Nothing, however, all the doctors, French and English, assured me, could have helped him to fight his disease, except a strong constitution. And his was so enfeebled by illness as to make the contest an unequal one. They gave us hardly any hope from the first.'

[2] The telegrams were received as if from Lemnos, and as there was no reason to suppose otherwise it was assumed, and published, that he had died there.

[3] This sentence is from the letter to Mrs Brooke.

BURIAL

'We buried him the same evening in an olive-grove where he had sat with us on Tuesday—one of the loveliest places on this earth, with grey-green olives round him, one weeping above his head; the ground covered with flowering sage, bluish-grey, and smelling more delicious than any flower I know. The path up to it from the sea is narrow and difficult and very stony; it runs by the bed of a dried-up torrent. We had to post men with lamps every twenty yards to guide the bearers. He was carried up from the boat by his A Company petty officers, led by his platoon-sergeant Saunders ; and it was with enormous difficulty that they got the coffin up the narrow way. The journey of a mile took two hours. It was not till 11 that I saw them coming (I had gone up to choose the place, and with Freyberg and Charles Lister I turned the sods of his grave; we had some of his platoon to dig). First came one of his men carrying a great white wooden cross with his name painted on it in black; then the firing-party, commanded by Patrick; and then the coffin, followed by our officers, and General Paris and one or two others of the Brigade. Think of it all under a clouded moon, with the three mountains[1] around and behind us, and those divine scents everywhere. We lined his grave with all the flowers we could find, and Quilter set a wreath of olive on the coffin. The funeral service was very simply said by the Chaplain, and after the Last Post the little lamp-lit procession went once again down the narrow path to the sea.

[1] Their names are Paphko, Komaro, and Khokilas.

'Freyberg, Oc, I, Charles and Cleg [Kelly] stayed behind and covered the grave with great pieces of white marble which were lying everywhere about. Of the cross at the head you know; it was the large one that headed the procession. On the back of it our Greek interpreter wrote in pencil:

ἐνθάδε κεῖται
ὁ δοῦλος τοῦ Θεοῦ
ἀνθυπολοχαγὸς τοῦ
'Αγγλικοῦ ναυτικοῦ
ἀποθανὼν ὑπὲρ τῆς
ἀπελευθερώσεως τῆς
Κων· πούλεως ἀπὸ
τῶν Τουρκῶν.[1]

At his feet was a small wooden cross sent by his platoon. We could not see the grave again, as we sailed from Scyros next morning at 6.'

The same friend wrote to Mrs Brooke: 'No words of mine can tell you the sorrow of those whom he has left behind him here. No one of us knew him without loving him, whether they knew him for ten years, as I did, or for a couple of months as others. His brother officers and his men mourn him very deeply. But those who knew him chiefly as a poet of the rarest gifts, the brightest genius, know that the loss is not only yours and ours, but the world's. And beyond his genius there was that infinitely lovable soul, that stain-

[1] Here lies the servant of God, Sub-Lieutenant in the English Navy, who died for the deliverance of Constantinople from the Turks.

less heart whose earthly death can only be the beginning of a true immortality.

'To his friends Rupert stood for something so much purer, greater, and nobler than ordinary men that his loss seems more explicable than theirs. He has gone to where he came from; but if anyone left the world richer by passing through it, it was he.'

Next morning the *Grantully Castle* sailed for the Gallipoli Peninsula. Within six weeks, of the officers named in Denis Browne's letter, he and Colonel Quilter were dead, and all but one of the others had been wounded. Kelly, Lister, and Shaw-Stewart have since been killed.

Winston Churchill wrote in *The Times* of April 26th: 'Rupert Brooke is dead. A telegram from the Admiral at Lemnos tells us that this life has closed at the moment when it seemed to have reached its springtime. A voice had become audible, a note had been struck, more true, more thrilling, more able to do justice to the nobility of our youth in arms engaged in this present war, than any other—more able to express their thoughts of self-surrender, and with a power to carry comfort to those who watched them so intently from afar. The voice has been swiftly stilled. Only the echoes and the memory remain; but they will linger.

'During the last few months of his life, months of preparation in gallant comradeship and open air, the poet-soldier told with all the simple force of genius the sorrow of youth about to die, and the sure triumphant consolations of a sincere and valiant spirit. He expected to die; he was willing to die for the dear England whose beauty and majesty he knew; and he advanced towards the brink in perfect serenity, with absolute conviction of the rightness of his country's cause, and a heart devoid of hate for fellow-men.

'The thoughts to which he gave expression in the very few incomparable war sonnets which he has left behind will be shared by many thousands of young men moving resolutely and blithely forward into this, the hardest, the cruellest, and the least-rewarded of all the wars that men have fought. They are a whole history and revelation of Rupert Brooke himself. Joyous, fearless, versatile, deeply instructed, with classic symmetry of mind and body, he was all that one would wish England's noblest sons to be in days when no sacrifice but the most precious is acceptable, and the most precious is that which is most freely proffered.'

*   *   *

'Coming from Alexandria yesterday,' Denis Browne wrote to me on June 2nd, two days before his own death, 'we passed Rupert's island at sunset. The sea and sky in the East were grey and misty; but it stood out in the West, black and immense, with a crimson glowing halo round it. Every colour had come into the sea and sky to do him honour; and it seemed that the island must ever be shining with his glory that we buried there.'

POEMS 1905–1911

1905–1908

SECOND BEST

Here in the dark, O heart;
Alone with the enduring Earth, and Night,
And Silence, and the warm strange smell of clover;
Clear-visioned, though it break you; far apart
From the dead best, the dear and old delight;
Throw down your dreams of immortality,
O faithful, O foolish lover!
Here's peace for you, and surety; here the one
Wisdom—the truth!—'All day the good glad sun
Showers love and labour on you, wine and song;
The greenwood laughs, the wind blows, all day long
Till night.' And night ends all things.
                                        Then shall be
No lamp relumed in heaven, no voices crying,
Or changing lights, or dreams and forms that hover!
(And, heart, for all your sighing,
That gladness and those tears are over, over. . . .)

And has the truth brought no new hope at all,
Heart, that you're weeping yet for Paradise?
Do they still whisper, the old weary cries?
"Mid youth and song, feasting and carnival,
Through laughter, through the roses, as of old
Comes Death, on shadowy and relentless feet,
Death, unappeasable by prayer or gold;
Death is the end, the end!"
Proud, then, clear-eyed and laughing, go to greet
Death as a friend!

Exile of immortality, strongly wise,
Strain through the dark with undesirous eyes
To what may lie beyond it. Sets your star,
O heart, for ever! Yet, behind the night,
Waits for the great unborn, somewhere afar,
Some white tremendous daybreak. And the light,
Returning, shall give back the golden hours,
Ocean a windless level, Earth a lawn
Spacious and full of sunlit dancing-places,
And laughter, and music, and, among the flowers,
The gay child-hearts of men, and the child-faces,
O heart, in the great dawn!

1908

DAY THAT I HAVE LOVED

Tenderly, day that I have loved, I close your eyes,
  And smooth your quiet brow, and fold your thin
    dead hands.
The grey veils of the half-light deepen; colour dies.
  I bear you, a light burden, to the shrouded sands,

Where lies your waiting boat, by wreaths of the sea's
    making
  Mist-garlanded, with all grey weeds of the water
    crowned.
There you'll be laid, past fear of sleep or hope of
    waking;
  And over the unmoving sea, without a sound,

Faint hands will row you outward, out beyond our
    sight,
  Us with stretched arms and empty eyes on the
    far-gleaming
And marble sand. . . .
                Beyond the shifting cold twilight,
  Further than laughter goes, or tears, further than
    dreaming,

There'll be no port, no dawn-lit islands! But the drear
  Waste darkening, and, at length, flame ultimate on
    the deep.
Oh, the last fire—and you, unkissed, unfriended
    there!
  Oh, the lone way's red ending, and we not there to
    weep!

(We found you pale and quiet, and strangely crowned
    with flowers,
  Lovely and secret as a child. You came with us,
Came happily, hand in hand with the young dancing
    hours,
  High on the downs at dawn!) Void now and
    tenebrous,

The grey sands curve before me. . . .
                    From the inland meadows,
  Fragrant of June and clover, floats the dark, and
    fills
The hollow sea's dead face with little creeping
    shadows,
  And the white silence brims the hollow of the hills.

Close in the nest is folded every weary wing,
  Hushed all the joyful voices; and we, who held you
    dear,
Eastward we turn and homeward, alone,
    remembering . . .
  Day that I loved, day that I loved, the Night is here!

They sleep within. . . .
I cower to the earth, I waking, I only.
High and cold thou dreamest, O queen,
  high-dreaming and lonely.

We have slept too long, who can hardly win
The white one flame, and the night-long crying;
The viewless passers; the world's low sighing
With desire, with yearning,
To the fire unburning,
To the heatless fire, to the flameless ecstasy! . . .

Helpless I lie.
And around me the feet of thy watchers tread.
There is a rumour and a radiance of wings above my
  head,
An intolerable radiance of wings. . . .

All the earth grows fire,
White lips of desire
Brushing cool on the forehead, croon slumbrous
  things.
Earth fades; and the air is thrilled with ways,
Dewy paths full of comfort. And radiant bands,
The gracious presence of friendly hands,
Help the blind one, the glad one, who stumbles and
  strays,
Stretching wavering hands, up, up, through the praise

Of a myriad silver trumpets, through cries,
To all glory, to all gladness, to the infinite height,
To the gracious, the unmoving, the mother eyes,
And the laughter, and the lips, of light.

August 1908

IN EXAMINATION

Lo! from quiet skies
In through the window my Lord the Sun!
And my eyes
Were dazzled and drunk with the misty gold,
The golden glory that drowned and crowned me
Eddied and swayed through the room . . .
                                        Around me,
To left and to right,
Hunched figures and old,
Dull blear-eyed scribbling fools, grew fair,
Ringed round and haloed with holy light.
Flame lit on their hair,
And their burning eyes grew young and wise,
Each as a God, or King of kings,
White-robed and bright
(Still scribbling all);
And a full tumultuous murmur of wings
Grew through the hall;
And I knew the white undying Fire,
And, through open portals,
Gyre on gyre,
Archangels and angels, adoring, bowing,
And a Face unshaded. . . .
Till the light faded;
And they were but fools again, fools unknowing,
Still scribbling, blear-eyed and stolid immortals.

   10 *November* 1908

PINE-TREES AND THE SKY:
EVENING

I'd watched the sorrow of the evening sky,
And smelt the sea, and earth, and the warm clover,
And heard the waves, and the seagull's mocking cry.

And in them all was only the old cry,
That song they always sing—'The best is over!
You may remember now, and think, and sigh,
O silly lover!'
And I was tired and sick that all was over,
And because I,
For all my thinking, never could recover
One moment of the good hours that were over.
And I was sorry and sick, and wished to die.

Then from the sad west turning wearily,
I saw the pines against the white north sky,
Very beautiful, and still, and bending over
Their sharp black heads against a quiet sky.
And there was peace in them; and I
Was happy, and forgot to play the lover,
And laughed, and did no longer wish to die;
Being glad of you, O pine-trees and the sky!

L U L W O R T H, 8 *July* 1907

WAGNER

Creeps in half wanton, half asleep,
  One with a fat wide hairless face.
He likes love-music that is cheap;
  Likes women in a crowded place;
    And wants to hear the noise they're making.

His heavy eyelids droop half-over,
  Great pouches swing beneath his eyes.
He listens, thinks himself the lover,
  Heaves from his stomach wheezy sighs;
    He likes to feel his heart's a-breaking.

The music swells. His gross legs quiver.
  His little lips are bright with slime.
The music swells. The women shiver.
  And all the while, in perfect time,
    His pendulous stomach hangs a-shaking.

QUEEN'S HALL, 1908

181

THE VISION OF THE ARCHANGELS

Slowly up silent peaks, the white edge of the world,
  Trod four archangels, clear against the unheeding
    sky,
Bearing, with quiet even steps, and great wings furled,
  A little dingy coffin; where a child must lie,
It was so tiny. (Yet, you had fancied, God could never
  Have bidden a child turn from the spring and the
    sunlight,
And shut him in that lonely shell, to drop for ever
  Into the emptiness and silence, into the night. . . .)

They then from the sheer summit cast, and watched it
    fall,
  Through unknown glooms, that frail black coffin—
    and therein
  God's little pitiful Body lying, worn and thin,
And curled up like some crumpled, lonely
    flower-petal—
Till it was no more visible; then turned again
With sorrowful quiet faces downward to the plain.

December 1906

SEASIDE

Swiftly out from the friendly lilt of the band,
  The crowd's good laughter, the loved eyes of men
  I am drawn nightward; I must turn again
Where, down beyond the low untrodden strand,
There curves and glimmers outward to the unknown
  The old unquiet ocean. All the shade
Is rife with magic and movement. I stray alone
  Here on the edge of silence, half afraid,

Waiting a sign. In the deep heart of me
The sullen waters swell towards the moon,
And all my tides set seaward.
                From inland
Leaps a gay fragment of some mocking tune,
That tinkles and laughs and fades along the sand,
And dies between the seawall and the sea.

ON THE DEATH OF SMET-SMET, THE HIPPOPOTAMUS GODDESS

SONG OF A TRIBE OF THE ANCIENT EGYPTIANS

(*The Priests within the Temple*)

She was wrinkled and huge and hideous? She was our
Mother.
She was lustful and lewd?—but a God; we had none
other.
In the day She was hidden and dumb, but at nightfall
moaned in the shade;
We shuddered and gave Her Her will in the darkness;
we were afraid.

(*The People without*)

> *She sent us pain,*
> *And we bowed before Her;*
> *She smiled again*
> *And bade us adore Her.*
> *She solaced our woe*
> *And soothed our sighing;*
> *And what shall we do*
> *Now God is dying?*

(*The Priests within*)

She was hungry and ate our children;—how should
we stay Her?
She took our young men and our maidens;—ours to
obey Her.

We were loathèd and mocked and reviled of all na-
tions; that was our pride.
She fed us, protected us, loved us, and killed us; now
She has died.

(*The People without*)

> *She was so strong;*
> *But Death is stronger.*
> *She ruled us long;*
> *But Time is longer.*
> *She solaced our woe*
> *And soothed our sighing;*
> *And what shall we do*
> *Now God is dying?*

1908

THE SONG OF THE PILGRIMS

*(Halted around the fire by night, after moon-set, they
sing this beneath the trees)*

What light of unremembered skies
Hast thou relumed within our eyes,
Thou whom we seek, whom we shall find? . . .
A certain odour on the wind,
Thy hidden face beyond the west,
These things have called us; on a quest
Older than any road we trod,
More endless than desire. . . .
                           Far God,
Sigh with thy cruel voice, that fills
The soul with longing for dim hills
And faint horizons! For there come
Grey moments of the antient dumb
Sickness of travel, when no song
Can cheer us; but the way seems long;
And one remembers. . . .
                           Ah! the beat
Of weary unreturning feet,
And songs of pilgrims unreturning! . . .
The fires we left are always burning
On the old shrines of home. Our kin
Have built them temples, and therein
Pray to the Gods we know; and dwell
In little houses lovable,
Being happy (we remember how!)
And peaceful even to death. . . .

                                        O Thou,
God of all long desirous roaming,
Our hearts are sick of fruitless homing,
And crying after lost desire.
Hearten us onward! as with fire
Consuming dreams of other bliss.
The best Thou givest, giving this
Sufficient thing—to travel still
Over the plain, beyond the hill,
Unhesitating through the shade,
Amid the silence unafraid,
Till, at some sudden turn, one sees
Against the black and muttering trees
Thine altar, wonderfully white,
Among the Forests of the Night.

   1907

THE SONG OF THE BEASTS

(Sung, on one night, in the cities, in the darkness)

Come away! Come away!
Ye are sober and dull through the common day,
But now it is night!
It is shameful night, and God is asleep!
(Have you not felt the quick fires that creep
Through the hungry flesh, and the lust of delight,
And hot secrets of dreams that day cannot say?). . .
. . . The house is dumb;
The night calls out to you. . . . Come, ah, come!
Down the dim stairs, through the creaking door,
Naked, crawling on hands and feet
—It is meet! it is meet!
Ye are men no longer, but less and more,
Beast and God. . . . Down the lampless street,
By little black ways, and secret places,
In darkness and mire,
Faint laughter around, and evil faces
By the star-glint seen—ah! follow with us!
For the darkness whispers a blind desire,
And the fingers of night are amorous. . . .
Keep close as we speed,
Though mad whispers woo you, and hot hands cling,
And the touch and the smell of bare flesh sting,
Soft flank by your flank, and side brushing side—
Tonight never heed!
Unswerving and silent follow with me,
Till the city ends sheer,

And the crook'd lanes open wide,
Out of the voices of night,
Beyond lust and fear,
To the level waters of moonlight,
To the level waters, quiet and clear,
To the black unresting plains of the calling sea.

1906

FAILURE

Because God put His adamantine fate
    Between my sullen heart and its desire,
I swore that I would burst the Iron Gate,
    Rise up, and curse Him on His throne of fire.
Earth shuddered at my crown of blasphemy,
    But Love was as a flame about my feet;
    Proud up the Golden Stair I strode; and beat
Thrice on the Gate, and entered with a cry—

All the great courts were quiet in the sun,
    And full of vacant echoes: moss had grown
Over the glassy pavement, and begun
    To creep within the dusty council-halls.
An idle wind blew round an empty throne
    And stirred the heavy curtains on the walls.

ANTE ARAM

Before thy shrine I kneel, an unknown worshipper,
   Chanting strange hymns to thee and sorrowful
   litanies,
Incense of dirges, prayers that are as holy myrrh.

Ah! goddess, on thy throne of tears and faint low
   sighs,
   Weary at last to theeward come the feet that err,
And empty hearts grown tired of the world's vanities.

How fair this cool deep silence to a wanderer[1]
   Deaf with the roar of winds along the open skies!
Sweet, after sting and bitter kiss of sea-water,

The pale Lethean wine within thy chalices! . . .
   I come before thee, I, too tired wanderer
To heed the horror of the shrine, the distant cries,

And evil whispers in the gloom, or the swift whirr
   Of terrible wings—I, least of all thy votaries,
With a faint hope to see the scented darkness stir,

And, parting, frame within its quiet mysteries
   One face, with lips than autumn-lilies tenderer,
And voice more sweet than the far plaint of viols is,

   Or the soft moan of any grey-eyed lute-player.

[1] I think the poet must have meant to write 'wayfarer' either
here or in line 11.—E. M.

DAWN

*(From the train between Bologna and Milan,
second class)*

Opposite me two Germans snore and sweat.
   Through sullen swirling gloom we jolt and roar.
We have been here for ever: even yet
   A dim watch tells two hours, two æons, more.
The windows are tight-shut and slimy-wet
   With a night's fœtor. There are two hours more;
Two hours to dawn and Milan; two hours yet.
   Opposite me two Germans sweat and snore. . . .

One of them wakes, and spits, and sleeps again.
   The darkness shivers. A wan light through the rain
Strikes on our faces, drawn and white. Somewhere
   A new day sprawls; and, inside, the foul air
Is chill, and damp, and fouler than before. . . .
   Opposite me two Germans sweat and snore.

THE CALL

Out of the nothingness of sleep,
  The slow dreams of Eternity,
There was a thunder on the deep:
  I came, because you called to me.

I broke the Night's primeval bars,
  I dared the old abysmal curse,
And flashed through ranks of frightened stars
  Suddenly on the universe!

The eternal silences were broken;
  Hell became Heaven as I passed.—
What shall I give you as a token,
  A sign that we have met, at last?

I'll break and forge the stars anew,
  Shatter the heavens with a song;
Immortal in my love for you,
  Because I love you, very strong.

Your mouth shall mock the old and wise,
  Your laugh shall fill the world with flame,
I'll write upon the shrinking skies
  The scarlet splendour of your name,

Till Heaven cracks, and Hell thereunder
  Dies in her ultimate made fire,
And darkness falls, with scornful thunder,
  On dreams of men and men's desire.

Then only in the empty spaces,
    Death, walking very silently,
Shall fear the glory of our faces
    Through all the dark infinity.

So, clothed about with perfect love,
    The eternal end shall find us one,
Alone above the Night, above
    The dust of the dead gods, alone.

THE WAYFARERS

Is it the hour? We leave this resting-place
   Made fair by one another for a while.
Now, for a god-speed, one last mad embrace;
   The long road then, unlit by your faint smile.
Ah! the long road! and you so far away!
Oh, I'll remember! but . . . each crawling day
   Will pale a little your scarlet lips, each mile
Dull the dear pain of your remembered face.

. . . Do you think there's a far border town,
     somewhere,
   The desert's edge, last of the lands we know,
    Some gaunt eventual limit of our light,
   In which I'll find you waiting; and we'll go
Together, hand in hand again, out there,
    Into the waste we know not, into the night?

THE BEGINNING

Some day I shall rise and leave my friends
And seek you again through the world's far ends,
You whom I found so fair,
(Touch of your hands and smell of your hair!),
My only god in the days that were.
My eager feet shall find you again,
Though the sullen years and the mark of pain
Have changed you wholly; for I shall know
(How could I forget having loved you so?),
In the sad half-light of evening,
The face that was all my sunrising.
So then at the ends of the earth I'll stand
And hold you fiercely by either hand,
And seeing your age and ashen hair
I'll curse the thing that once you were,
Because it is changed and pale and old
(Lips that were scarlet, hair that was gold!),
And I loved you before you were old and wise,
When the flame of youth was strong in your eyes,
  —And my heart is sick with memories.

1906

EXPERIMENTS

CHORIAMBICS · I

Ah! not now, when desire burns, and the wind calls,
    and the suns of spring
Light-foot dance in the woods, whisper of life, woo
    me to wayfaring:
Ah! not now should you come, now when the road
    beckons, and good friends call,
Where are songs to be sung, fights to be fought, yea!
    and the best of all,
Love, on myriad lips fairer than yours, kisses you
    could not give! . . .
Dearest, why should I mourn, whimper, and whine,
    I that have yet to live?
Sorrow will I forget, tears for the best, love on the
    lips of you,
Now, when dawn in the blood wakes, and the sun
    laughs up the eastern blue;
I'll forget and be glad!
        Only at length, dear, when the great day ends,
When love dies with the last light, and the last song
    has been sung, and friends
All are perished, and gloom strides on the heaven:
    then, as alone I lie,
'Mid Death's gathering winds, frightened and dumb,
    sick for the past, may I
Feel you suddenly there, cool at my brow; then may
    I hear the peace
Of your voice at the last, whispering love, calling, ere
    all can cease

In the silence of death; then may I see dimly, and
    know, a space,
Bending over me, last light in the dark, once, as of old,
    your face.

December 1908

Here the flame that was ash, shrine that was void, lost
    in the haunted wood,
I have tended and loved, year upon year, I in the
    solitude
Waiting, quiet and glad-eyed in the dark, knowing
    that once a gleam
Glowed and went through the wood. Still I abode
    strong in a golden dream,
Unrecaptured.
            For I, I that had faith, knew that a face
               would glance
One day, white in the dim woods, and a voice call,
    and a radiance
Fill the grove, and the fire suddenly leap . . . and, in
    the heart of it,
End of labouring, you! Therefore I kept ready the
    altar, lit
The flame, burning apart.
              Face of my dreams vainly in vision white
Gleaming down to me, lo! hopeless I rise now. For
    about midnight
Whispers grew through the wood suddenly, strange
    cries in the boughs above
Grated, cries like a laugh. Silent and black then
    through the sacred grove
Great birds flew, as a dream, troubling the leaves,
    passing at length.

I knew,
Long expected and long loved, that afar, God of the
dim wood, you
Somewhere lay, as a child sleeping, a child suddenly
reft from mirth.
White and wonderful yet, white in your youth,
stretched upon foreign earth,
God, immortal and dead!
Therefore I go; never to rest, or win
Peace, and worship of you more, and the dumb wood
and the shrine therein.

December 1908

DESERTION

So light we were, so right we were, so fair faith
 shone,
And the way was laid so certainly, that, when I'd
 gone,
What dumb thing looked up at you? Was it some-
 thing heard,
Or a sudden cry, that meekly and without a word
You broke the faith, and strangely, weakly, slipped
 apart?
You gave in—you, the proud of heart, unbowed of
 heart!
Was this, friend, the end of all that we could do?
And have you found the best for you, the rest for
 you?
Did you learn so suddenly (and I not by!)
Some whispered story, that stole the glory from the
 sky,
And ended all the splendid dream, and made you go
So dully from the fight we know, the light we know?

O faithless! the faith remains, and I must pass
Gay down the way, and on alone. Under the grass
You wait; the breeze moves in the trees, and stirs, and
 calls,
And covers you with white petals, with light petals.

There it shall crumble, frail and fair, under the sun,
O little heart, your brittle heart; till day be done,
And the shadows gather, falling light, and, white with
  dew,
Whisper, and weep; and creep to you. Good sleep to
  you!

March 1910

1908–1911

SONNET

Oh! Death will find me, long before I tire
    Of watching you; and swing me suddenly
Into the shade and loneliness and mire
    Of the last land! There, waiting patiently,

One day, I think, I'll feel a cool wind blowing,
    See a slow light across the Stygian tide,
And hear the Dead about me stir, unknowing,
    And tremble. And *I* shall know that you have died,

And watch you, a broad-browed and smiling dream,
    Pass, light as ever, through the lightless host,
Quietly ponder, start, and sway, and gleam—
    Most individual and bewildering ghost!—

And turn, and toss your brown delightful head
Amusedly, among the ancient Dead.

April 1909

SONNET

I said I splendidly loved you; it's not true.
    Such long swift tides stir not a land-locked sea.
On gods or fools the high risk falls—on you—
    The clean clear bitter-sweet that's not for me.
Love soars from earth to ecstacies unwist.
    Love is flung Lucifer-like from Heaven to Hell.
But—there are wanderers in the middle mist,
    Who cry for shadows, clutch, and cannot tell
Whether they love at all, or, loving, whom:
    An old song's lady, a fool in fancy dress,
Or phantoms, or their own face on the gloom;
    For love of Love, or from heart's loneliness.
Pleasure's not theirs, nor pain. They doubt, and sigh
And do not love at all. Of these am I.

January 1910

SUCCESS

I think if you had loved me when I wanted;
　　If I'd looked up one day, and seen your eyes,
And found my wild sick blasphemous prayer granted,
　　And your brown face, that's full of pity and wise,
Flushed suddenly; the white godhead in new fear
　　Intolerably so struggling, and so shamed;
Most holy and far, if you'd come all too near,
　　If earth had seen Earth's lordliest wild limbs tamed,
Shaken, and trapped, and shivering, for *my* touch—
　　Myself should I have slain? or that foul you?
But this the strange gods, who had given so much,
　　To have seen and known you, this they might not
　　　　do.
One last shame's spared me, one black word's un-
　　spoken;
And I'm alone; and you have not awoken.

January 1910

DUST

When the white flame in us is gone,
　And we that lost the world's delight
Stiffen in darkness, left alone
　To crumble in our separate night;

When your swift hair is quiet in death,
　And through the lips corruption thrust
Has stilled the labour of my breath—
　When we are dust, when we are dust!—

Not dead, not undesirous yet,
　Still sentient, still unsatisfied,
We'll ride the air, and shine, and flit,
　Around the places where we died,

And dance as dust before the sun,
　And light of foot, and unconfined,
Hurry from road to road, and run
　About the errands of the wind.

And every mote, on earth or air,
　Will speed and gleam, down later days,
And like a secret pilgrim fare
　By eager and invisible ways,

Nor ever rest, nor ever lie,
　Till, beyond thinking, out of view,
One mote of all the dust that's I
　Shall meet one atom that was you.

Then in some garden hushed from wind,
    Warm in a sunset's afterglow,
The lovers in the flowers will find
    A sweet and strange unquiet grow

Upon the peace; and, past desiring,
    So high a beauty in the air,
And such a light, and such a quiring,
    And such a radiant ecstasy there,

They'll know not if it's fire, or dew,
    Or out of earth, or in the height,
Singing, or flame, or scent, or hue,
    Or two that pass, in light, to light.

Out of the garden higher, higher. . . .
    But in that instant they shall learn
The shattering ecstasy of our fire,
    And the weak passionless hearts will burn

And faint in that amazing glow,
    Until the darkness close above;
And they will know—poor fools, they'll
        know!—
    One moment, what it is to love.

December 1909–*March* 1910

KINDLINESS

When love has changed to kindliness—
Oh, love, our hungry lips, that press
So tight that Time's an old god's dream
Nodding in heaven, and whisper stuff
Seven million years were not enough
To think on after, make it seem
Less than the breath of children playing,
A blasphemy scarce worth the saying,
A sorry jest, 'When love has grown
To kindliness—to kindliness!'...
And yet—the best that either's known
Will change, and wither, and be less,
At last, than comfort, or its own
Remembrance. And when some caress
Tendered in habit (once a flame
All heaven sang out to) wakes the shame
Unworded, in the steady eyes
We'll have,—*that* day, what shall we do?
Being so noble, kill the two
Who've reached their second-best? Being wise,
Break cleanly off, and get away,
Follow down other windier skies
New lures, alone? Or shall we stay,
Since this is all we've known, content
In the lean twilight of such day,
And not remember, not lament?
That time when all is over, and
Hand never flinches, brushing hand;

And blood lies quiet, for all you're near;
And it's but spoken words we hear,
Where trumpets sang; when the mere skies
Are stranger and nobler than your eyes;
And flesh is flesh, was flame before;
And infinite hungers leap no more
In the chance swaying of your dress;
And love has changed to kindliness.

MUMMIA

As those of old drank mummia
  To fire their limbs of lead,
Making dead kings from Africa
  Stand pandar to their bed;

Drunk on the dead, and medicined
  With spiced imperial dust,
In a short night they reeled to find
  Ten centuries of lust.

So I, from paint, stone, tale, and rhyme,
  Stuffed love's infinity,
And sucked all lovers of all time
  To rarefy ecstasy.

Helen's the hair shuts out from me
  Verona's livid skies;
Gypsy the lips I press; and see
  Two Antonys in your eyes.

The unheard invisible lovely dead
  Lie with us in this place,
And ghostly hands above my head
  Close face to straining face;

Their blood is wine along our limbs;
  Their whispering voices wreathe
Savage forgotten drowsy hymns
  Under the names we breathe;

Woven from their tomb, and one with it,
  The night wherein we press;
Their thousand pitchy pyres have lit
  Your flaming nakedness.

For the uttermost years have cried and clung
  To kiss your mouth to mine;
And hair long dust was caught, was flung,
  Hand shaken to hand divine,

And Life has fired, and Death not shaded,
  All Time's uncounted bliss,
And the height o' the world has flamed and faded,—
  Love, that our love be this!

THE FISH

In a cool curving world he lies
And ripples with dark ecstasies.
The kind luxurious lapse and steal
Shapes all his universe to feel
And know and be; the clinging stream
Closes his memory, glooms his dream,
Who lips the roots o' the shore, and glides
Superb on unreturning tides.
Those silent waters weave for him
A fluctuant mutable world and dim,
Where wavering masses bulge and gape
Mysterious, and shape to shape
Dies momently through whorl and hollow,
And form and line and solid follow
Solid and line and form to dream
Fantastic down the eternal stream;
An obscure world, a shifting world,
Bulbous, or pulled to thin, or curled,
Or serpentine, or driving arrows,
Or serene slidings, or March narrows.
There slipping wave and shore are one,
And weed and mud. No ray of sun,
But glow to glow fades down the deep
(As dream to unknown dream in sleep);
Shaken translucency illumes
The hyaline of drifting glooms;
The strange soft-handed depth subdues
Drowned colour there, but black to hues,

As death to living, decomposes—
Red darkness of the heart of roses,
Blue brilliant from dead starless skies,
And gold that lies behind the eyes,
The unknown unnameable sightless white
That is the essential flame of night,
Lustreless purple, hooded green,
The myriad hues that lie between
Darkness and darkness! . . .

                  And all's one
Gentle, embracing, quiet, dun,
The world he rests in, world he knows,
Perpetual curving. Only—grows
An eddy in that ordered falling,
A knowledge from the gloom, a calling
Weed in the wave, gleam in the mud—
The dark fire leaps along his blood;
Dateless and deathless, blind and still,
The intricate impulse works its will;
His woven world drops back; and he,
Sans providence, sans memory,
Unconscious and directly driven,
Fades to some dank sufficient heaven.

O world of lips, O world of laughter,
Where hope is fleet and thought flies after,
Of lights in the clear night, of cries
That drift along the wave and rise

Thin to the glittering stars above,
You know the hands, the eyes of love!
The strife of limbs, the sightless clinging,
The infinite distance, and the singing
Blown by the wind, a flame of sound,
The gleam, the flowers, and vast around
The horizon, and the heights above—
You know the sigh, the song of love!

But there the night is close, and there
Darkness is cold and strange and bare;
And the secret deeps are whisperless;
And rhythm is all deliciousness;
And joy is in the throbbing tide,
Whose intricate fingers beat and glide
In felt bewildering harmonies
Of trembling touch; and music is
The exquisite knocking of the blood.
Space is no more, under the mud;
His bliss is older than the sun.
Silent and straight the waters run.
The lights, the cries, the willows dim,
And the dark tide are one with him.

MUNICH, *March* 1911

THOUGHTS ON THE SHAPE OF
THE HUMAN BODY

How can we find? how can we rest? how can
We, being gods, win joy, or peace, being man?
We, the gaunt zanies of a witless Fate,
Who love the unloving, and the lover hate,
Forget the moment ere the moment slips,
Kiss with blind lips that seek beyond the lips,
Who want, and know not what we want, and cry
With crooked mouths for Heaven, and throw it by.
Love's for completeness! No perfection grows
'Twixt leg, and arm, elbow, and ear, and nose,
And joint, and socket; but unsatisfied
Sprawling desires, shapeless, perverse, denied.
Finger with finger wreathes; we love, and gape,
Fantastic shape to mazed fantastic shape,
Straggling, irregular, perplexed, embossed,
Grotesquely twined, extravagantly lost
By crescive paths and strange protuberant ways
From sanity and from wholeness and from grace.
How can love triumph, how can solace be,
Where fever turns toward fever, knee toward knee?
Could we but fill to harmony, and dwell
Simple as our thought and as perfectible,
Rise disentangled from humanity
Strange whole and new into simplicity,
Grow to a radiant round love, and bear
Unfluctuant passion for some perfect sphere,

Love moon to moon unquestioning, and be
Like the star Lunisequa, steadfastly
Following the round clear orb of her delight,
Patiently ever, through the eternal night!

FLIGHT

Voices out of the shade that cried,
  And long noon in the hot calm places,
And children's play by the wayside,
  And country eyes, and quiet faces—
  All these were round my steady paces.

Those that I could have loved went by me;
  Cool gardened homes slept in the sun;
I heard the whisper of water nigh me,
  Saw hands that beckoned, shone, were gone
  In the green and gold. And I went on.

For if my echoing footfall slept,
  Soon a far whispering there'd be
Of a little lonely wind that crept
  From tree to tree, and distantly
  Followed me, followed me. . . .

But the blue vaporous end of day
  Brought peace, and pursuit baffled quite,
Where between pine-woods dipped the way.
  I turned, slipped in and out of sight.
  I trod as quiet as the night.

The pine-boles kept perpetual hush;
  And in the boughs wind never swirled.
I found a flowering lowly bush,
  And bowed, slid in, and sighed and curled,
  Hidden at rest from all the world.

Safe! I was safe, and glad, I knew!
    Yet—with cold heart and cold wet brows
I lay. And the dark fell. . . . There grew
    Meward a sound of shaken boughs;
    And ceased, above my intricate house;

And silence, silence, silence found me. . . .
    I felt the unfaltering movement creep
Among the leaves. They shed around me
    Calm clouds of scent, that I did weep,
    And stroked my face. I fell asleep.

1910

THE HILL

Breathless, we flung us on the windy hill,
  Laughed in the sun, and kissed the lovely grass.
  You said, 'Through glory and ecstasy we pass;
Wind, sun, and earth remain, the birds sing still,
When we are old, are old. . . .' 'And when we die
  All's over that is ours; and life burns on
Through other lovers, other lips,' said I,
  'Heart of my heart, our heaven is now, is won!'

'We are Earth's best, that learnt her lesson here.
  Life is our cry. We have kept the faith!' we said;
  'We shall go down with unreluctant tread
Rose-crowned into the darkness!' . . . Proud we
    were,
And laughed, that had such brave true things to say.
—And then you suddenly cried, and turned away.

1910

ı dreamt I was in love again
   With the One Before the Last,
And smiled to greet the pleasant pain
   Of that innocent young past.

But I jumped to feel how sharp had been
   The pain when it did live,
How the faded dreams of Nineteen-ten
   Were Hell in Nineteen-five.

The boy's woe was as keen and clear,
   The boy's love just as true,
And the One Before the Last, my dear,
   Hurt quite as much as you.

*   *   *

Sickly I pondered how the lover
   Wrongs the unanswering tomb,
And sentimentalizes over
   What earned a better doom.

Gently he tombs the poor dim last time,
   Strews pinkish dust above,
And sighs, 'The dear dead boyish pastime!
   But *this*—ah, God!—is Love!'

—Better oblivion hide dead true loves,
 Better the night enfold,
Than men, to eke the praise of new loves,
 Should lie about the old!

*　　*　　*

Oh! bitter thoughts I had in plenty.
 But here's the worst of it—
I shall forget, in Nineteen-twenty,
 You ever hurt a bit!

11 *January* 1910

THE JOLLY COMPANY

The stars, a jolly company,
　　I envied, straying late and lonely;
And cried upon their revelry:
　　'O white companionship! You only
In love, in faith unbroken dwell,
Friends radiant and inseparable!'

Light-heart and glad they seemed to me
　　And merry comrades (*even so*
God out of Heaven may laugh to see
　　The happy crowds; and never know
That in his lone obscure distress
Each walketh in a wilderness).

But I, remembering, pitied well
　　And loved them, who, with lonely light,
In empty infinite spaces dwell,
　　Disconsolate. For, all the night,
I heard the thin gnat-voices cry,
Star to faint star, across the sky.

November 1908

THE LIFE BEYOND

He wakes, who never thought to wake again,
    Who held the end was Death. He opens eyes
Slowly, to one long livid oozing plain
    Closed down by the strange eyeless heavens. He
        lies;
    And waits; and once in timeless sick surmise
Through the dead air heaves up an unknown hand,
Like a dry branch. No life is in that land,
    Himself not lives, but is a thing that cries;
An unmeaning point upon the mud; a speck
    Of moveless horror; an Immortal One
Cleansed of the world, sentient and dead; a fly
    Fast-stuck in grey sweat on a corpse's neck.

I thought when love for you died, I should die.
It's dead. Alone, most strangely, I live on.

April–September 1910

LINES WRITTEN IN THE BELIEF THAT THE ANCIENT ROMAN FESTIVAL OF THE DEAD WAS CALLED AMBARVALIA

Swings the way still by hollow and hill,
  And all the world's a song;
'She's far,' it sings me, 'but fair,' it rings me,
  'Quiet,' it laughs, 'and strong!'

Oh! spite of the miles and years between us,
  Spite of your chosen part,
I do remember; and I go
  With laughter in my heart.

So above the little folk that know not,
  Out of the white hill-town,
High up I clamber; and I remember;
  And watch the day go down.

Gold is my heart, and the world's golden,
  And one peak tipped with light;
And the air lies still about the hill
  With the first fear of night;

Till mystery down the soundless valley
  Thunders, and dark is here;
And the wind blows, and the light goes,
  And the night is full of fear.

And I know, one night, on some far height,
  In the tongue I never knew,
I yet shall hear the tidings clear
  From them that were friends of you.

They'll call the news from hill to hill,
  Dark and uncomforted,
Earth and sky and the winds; and I
  Shall know that you are dead.

I shall not hear your trentals,
  Nor eat your arval bread;
For the kin of you will surely do
  Their duty by the dead.

Their little dull greasy eyes will water;
  They'll paw you, and gulp afresh.
They'll sniffle and weep, and their thoughts will
    creep
  Like flies on the cold flesh.

They will put pence on your grey eyes,
  Bind up your fallen chin,
And lay you straight, the fools that loved you
  Because they were your kin.

They will praise all the bad about you,
  And hush the good away,
And wonder how they'll do without you,
  And then they'll go away.

But quieter than one sleeping,
  And stranger than of old,
You will not stir for weeping,
  You will not mind the cold;

But through the night the lips will laugh not,
  The hands will be in place,
And at length the hair be lying still
  About the quiet face.

With snuffle and sniff and handkerchief,
  And dim and decorous mirth,
With ham and sherry, they'll meet to bury
  The lordliest lass of earth.

The little dead hearts will tramp ungrieving
  Behind lone-riding you,
The heart so high, the heart so living,
  Heart that they never knew.

I shall not hear your trentals,
  Nor eat your arval bread,
Nor with smug breath tell lies of death
  To the unanswering dead.

With snuffle and sniff and handkerchief,
  The folk who loved you not
Will bury you, and go wondering
  Back home. And you will rot.

But laughing and half-way up to heaven,
  With wind and hill and star,
I yet shall keep, before I sleep,
  Your Ambarvalia.

There was a damned successful Poet;
　There was a Woman like the Sun.
And they were dead. They did not know it.
　They did not know their time was done.
　　They did not know his hymns
　　Were silence; and her limbs,
　　That had served Love so well,
　　Dust, and a filthy smell.

And so one day, as ever of old,
　Hands out, they hurried, knee to knee;
On fire to cling and kiss and hold
　And, in the other's eyes, to see
　　Each his own tiny face,
　　And in that long embrace
　　Feel lip and breast grow warm
　　To breast and lip and arm.

So knee to knee they sped again,
　And laugh to laugh they ran, I'm told,
Across the streets of Hell . . .
　　　　　　　　　And then
　They suddenly felt the wind blow cold,
　　And knew, so closely pressed,
　　Chill air on lip and breast,
　　And, with a sick surprise,
　　The emptiness of eyes.

MUNICH, 27 *February* 1911

TOWN AND COUNTRY

Here, where love's stuff is body, arm and side
  Are stabbing-sweet 'gainst chair and lamp and wall
In every touch more intimate meanings hide;
  And flaming brains are the white heart of all.

Here, million pulses to one centre beat:
  Closed in by men's vast friendliness, alone,
Two can be drunk with solitude, and meet
  On the sheer point where sense with knowing's one.

Here the green-purple clanging royal night,
  And the straight lines and silent walls of town,
And roar, and glare, and dust, and myriad white
  Undying passers, pinnacle and crown

Intensest heavens between close-lying faces
  By the lamp's airless fierce ecstatic fire;
And we've found love in little hidden places,
  Under great shades, between the mist and mire.

Stay! though the woods are quiet, and you've heard
  Night creep along the hedges. Never go
Where tangled foliage shrouds the crying bird,
  And the remote winds sigh, and waters flow!

Lest—as our words fall dumb on windless noons,
  Or hearts grow hushed and solitary, beneath
Unheeding stars and unfamiliar moons,
  Or boughs bend over, close and quiet as death,—

Unconscious and unpassionate and still,
   Cloud-like we lean and stare as bright leaves stare,
And gradually along the stranger hill
   Our unwalled loves thin out on vacuous air,

And suddenly there's no meaning in our kiss,
   And your lit upward face grows, where we lie,
Lonelier and dreadfuller than sunlight is,
   And dumb and mad and eyeless like the sky.

PARALYSIS

For moveless limbs no pity I crave,
  That never were swift! Still all I prize,
Laughter and thought and friends, I have;
  No fool to heave luxurious sighs
For the woods and hills that I never knew.
The more excellent way's yet mine! And you

Flower-laden come to the clean white cell,
  And we talk as ever—am I not the same?
With our hearts we love, immutable,
  You without pity, I without shame.
We talk as of old; as of old you go
Out under the sky, and laughing, I know,

Flit through the streets, your heart all me;
  Till you gain the world beyond the town.
Then—I fade from your heart, quietly;
  And your fleet steps quicken. The strong down
Smiles you welcome there; the woods that love you
Close lovely and conquering arms above you.

O ever-moving, O lithe and free!
  Fast in my linen prison I press
On impassable bars, or emptily
  Laugh in my great loneliness.
And still in the white neat bed I strive
Most impotently against that gyve;
Being less now than a thought, even,
To you alone with your hills and heaven.

  July 1909

233

I

Hot through Troy's ruin Menelaus broke
   To Priam's palace, sword in hand, to sate
   On that adulterous whore a ten years' hate
And a king's honour. Through red death, and smoke
And cries, and then by quieter ways he strode,
   Till the still innermost chamber fronted him.
   He swung his sword, and crashed into the dim
Luxurious bower, flaming like a god.

High sat white Helen, lonely and serene.
   He had not remembered that she was so fair
And that her neck curved down in such a way;
And he felt tired. He flung the sword away,
   And kissed her feet, and knelt before her there,
The perfect Knight before the perfect Queen.

So far the poet. How should he behold
That journey home, the long connubial years?
He does not tell you how white Helen bears
Child on legitimate child, becomes a scold,
Haggard with virtue. Menelaus bold
Waxed garrulous, and sacked a hundred Troys
'Twixt noon and supper. And her golden voice
Got shrill as he grew deafer. And both were old.

Often he wonders why on earth he went
Troyward, or why poor Paris ever came.
Oft she weeps, gummy-eyed and impotent;
Her dry shanks twitch at Paris' mumbled name.
So Menelaus nagged; and Helen cried;
And Paris slept on by Scamander side.

LUST

How should I know? The enormous wheels of will
   Drove me cold-eyed on tired and sleepless feet.
Night was void arms and you a phantom still,
   And day your far light swaying down the street.
As never fool for love, I starved for you;
   My throat was dry and my eyes hot to see.
Your mouth so lying was most heaven in view,
   And your remembered smell most agony.

Love wakens love! I felt your hot wrist shiver,
   And suddenly the mad victory I planned
     Flashed real, in your burning bending head. . . .
My conqueror's blood was cool as a deep river
   In shadow; and my heart beneath your hand
     Quieter than a dead man on a bed.

JEALOUSY

When I see you, who were so wise and cool,
Gazing with silly sickness on that fool
You've given your love to, your adoring hands
Touch his so intimately that each understands,
I know, most hidden things; and when I know
Your holiest dreams yield to the stupid bow
Of his red lips, and that the empty grace
Of those strong legs and arms, that rosy face,
Has beaten your heart to such a flame of love,
That you have given him every touch and move,
Wrinkle and secret of you, all your life,
—Oh! then I know I'm waiting, lover-wife,
For the great time when love is at a close,
And all its fruit's to watch the thickening nose
And sweaty neck and dulling face and eye,
That are yours, and you, most surely, till you die!
Day after day you'll sit with him and note
The greasier tie, the dingy wrinkling coat;
As prettiness turns to pomp, and strength to fat,
And love, love, love to habit!
       And after that,
When all that's fine in man is at an end,
And you, that loved young life and clean, must tend
A foul sick fumbling dribbling body and old,
When his rare lips hang flabby and can't hold
Slobber, and you're enduring that worst thing,
Senility's queasy furtive love-making,

And searching those dear eyes for human meaning,
Propping the bald and helpless head, and cleaning
A scrap that life's flung by, and love's forgotten,—
Then you'll be tired; and passion dead and rotten;
And he'll be dirty, dirty!
                              O lithe and free
And lightfoot, that the poor heart cries to see,
That's how I'll see your man and you!—

                                          But you
—Oh, when *that* time comes, you'll be dirty too!

BLUE EVENING

My restless blood now lies a-quiver,
  Knowing that always, exquisitely,
This April twilight on the river
  Stirs anguish in the heart of me.

For the fast world in that rare glimmer
  Puts on the witchery of a dream,
The straight grey buildings, richly dimmer,
  The fiery windows, and the stream

With willows leaning quietly over,
  The still ecstatic fading skies . . .
And all these, like a waiting lover,
  Murmur and gleam, lift lustrous eyes,

Drift close to me, and sideways bending
  Whisper delicious words.
                                But I
Stretch terrible hands, uncomprehending,
  Shaken with love; and laugh; and cry.

My agony made the willows quiver;
  I heard the knocking of my heart
Die loudly down the windless river,
  I heard the pale skies fall apart,

And the shrill stars' unmeaning laughter,
  And my voice with the vocal trees
Weeping. And Hatred followed after,
  Shrilling madly down the breeze.

In peace from the wild heart of clamour,
  A flower in moonlight, she was there,
Was rippling down white ways of glamour
  Quietly laid on wave and air.

Her passing left no leaf a-quiver.
  Pale flowers wreathed her white, white brows.
Her feet were silence on the river;
  And 'Hush!' she said, between the boughs.

May 1909

THE CHARM

In darkness the loud sea makes moan;
And earth is shaken, and all evils creep
About her ways.
                Oh, now to know you sleep!
Out of the whirling blinding moil, alone,
Out of the slow grim fight,
One thought to wing—to you, asleep,
In some cool room that's open to the night,
Lying half-forward, breathing quietly,
One white hand on the white
Unrumpled sheet, and the ever-moving hair
Quiet and still at length! . . .

Your magic and your beauty and your strength,
Like hills at noon or sunlight on a tree,
Sleeping prevail in earth and air.

In the sweet gloom above the brown and white
Night benedictions hover; and the winds of night
Move gently round the room, and watch you there,
And through the dreadful hours
The trees and waters and the hills have kept
The sacred vigil while you slept,
And lay a way of dew and flowers
Where your feet, your morning feet, shall tread.

And still the darkness ebbs about your bed.
Quiet, and strange, and loving-kind, you sleep.
And holy joy about the earth is shed;
And holiness upon the deep.

   8 *November* 1909

FINDING

From the candles and dumb shadows,
  And the house where love had died,
I stole to the vast moonlight
  And the whispering life outside.
But I found no lips of comfort,
  No home in the moon's light
(I, little and lone and frightened
  In the unfriendly night),
And no meaning in the voices. . . .
  Far over the lands, and through
The dark, beyond the ocean,
  I willed to think of *you*!
For I knew, had you been with me
  I'd have known the words of night,
Found peace of heart, gone gladly
  In comfort of that light.

Oh! the wind with soft beguiling
  Would have stolen my thought away
And the night, subtly smiling,
  Came by the silver way;
And the moon came down and danced to me,
  And her robe was white and flying;
And trees bent their heads to me
  Mysteriously crying;
And dead voices wept around me;
  And dead soft fingers thrilled;
And the little gods whispered. . . .

                              But ever
        Desperately I willed:
Till all grew soft and far
        And silent . . .
                         And suddenly
I found you white and radiant,
        Sleeping quietly,
Far out through the tides of darkness,
        And I there in that great light
Was alone no more, nor fearful;
        For there, in the homely night,
Was no thought else that mattered,
        And nothing else was true,
But the white fire of moonlight,
        And a white dream of you.

1909

SONG

'Oh! Love,' they said, 'is King of Kings,
   And Triumph is his crown.
Earth fades in flame before his wings,
   And Sun and Moon bow down.'—
But that, I knew, would never do;
   And Heaven is all too high.
So whenever I meet a Queen, I said,
   I will not catch her eye.

'Oh! Love,' they said, and 'Love,' they said,
   'The gift of Love is this;
A crown of thorns about thy head,
   And vinegar to thy kiss!'—
But Tragedy is not for me;
   And I'm content to be gay.
So whenever I spied a Tragic Lady,
   I went another way.

And so I never feared to see.
   You wander down the street,
Or come across the fields to me
   On ordinary feet.
For what they'd never told me of,
   And what I never knew;
It was that all the time, my love,
   Love would be merely you.

THE VOICE

Safe in the magic of my woods
  I lay, and watched the dying light.
Faint in the pale high solitudes,
  And washed with rain and veiled by night,

Silver and blue and green were showing.
  And the dark woods grew darker still;
And birds were hushed; and peace was growing;
  And quietness crept up the hill;

And no wind was blowing . . .

And I knew
That this was the hour of knowing,
And the night and the woods and you
Were one together, and I should find
Soon in the silence the hidden key
Of all that had hurt and puzzled me—
Why you were you, and the night was kind,
And the woods were part of the heart of me.

And there I waited breathlessly,
Alone; and slowly the holy three,
The three that I loved, together grew
One, in the hour of knowing,
Night, and the woods, and you——

And suddenly
There was an uproar in my woods,

The noise of a fool in mock distress,
Crashing and laughing and blindly going,
Of ignorant feet and a swishing dress,
And a Voice profaning the solitudes.

The spell was broken, the key denied me,
And at length your flat clear voice beside me
Mouthed cheerful clear flat platitudes.

You came and quacked beside me in the wood.
You said, 'The view from here is very good!'
You said, 'It's nice to be alone a bit!'
And, 'How the days are drawing out!' you said.
You said, 'The sunset's pretty, isn't it?'

*   *   *

By God! I wish—I wish that you were dead!

April 1909

DINING-ROOM TEA

When you were there, and you, and you,
Happiness crowned the night; I too,
Laughing and looking, one of all,
I watched the quivering lamplight fall
On plate and flowers and pouring tea
And cup and cloth; and they and we
Flung all the dancing moments by
With jest and glitter. Lip and eye
Flashed on the glory, shone and cried,
Improvident, unmemoried;
And fitfully and like a flame
The light of laughter went and came.
Proud in their careless transience moved
The changing faces that I loved.

Till suddenly, and otherwhence,
I looked upon your innocence.
For lifted clear and still and strange
From the dark woven flow of change
Under a vast and starless sky
I saw the immortal moment lie.
One instant I, an instant, knew
As God knows all. And it and you
I, above Time, oh, blind! could see
In witless immortality.
I saw the marble cup; the tea,
Hung on the air, an amber stream;
I saw the fire's unglittering gleam,

The painted flame, the frozen smoke.
No more the flooding lamplight broke
On flying eyes and lips and hair;
But lay, but slept unbroken there,
On stiller flesh, and body breathless,
And lips and laughter stayed and deathless,
And words on which no silence grew.
Light was more alive than you.

For suddenly, and otherwhence,
I looked on your magnificence.
I saw the stillness and the light,
And you, august, immortal, white,
Holy and strange; and every glint
Posture and jest and thought and tint
Freed from the mask of transiency,
Triumphant in eternity,
Immote, immortal.

                Dazed at length
Human eyes grew, mortal strength
Wearied; and Time began to creep.
Change closed about me like a sleep.
Light glinted on the eyes I loved.
The cup was filled. The bodies moved.
The drifting petal came to ground.
The laughter chimed its perfect round.
The broken syllable was ended.
And I, so certain and so friended,

How could I cloud, or how distress,
The heaven of your unconsciousness?
Or shake at Time's sufficient spell,
Stammering of lights unutterable?
The eternal holiness of you,
The timeless end, you never knew,
The peace that lay, the light that shone.
You never knew that I had gone
A million miles away, and stayed
A million years. The laughter played
Unbroken round me; and the jest
Flashed on. And we that knew the best
Down wonderful hours grew happier yet.
I sang at heart, and talked, and eat,
And lived from laugh to laugh, I too,
When you were there, and you, and you.

THE GODDESS IN THE WOOD

In a flowered dell the Lady Venus stood,
   Amazed with sorrow. Down the morning one
   Far golden horn in the gold of trees and sun
Rang out; and held; and died. . . . She thought the wood
Grew quieter. Wing, and leaf, and pool of light
   Forgot to dance. Dumb lay the unfalling stream;
   Life one eternal instant rose in dream
Clear out of time, poised on a golden height. . . .

Till a swift terror broke the abrupt hour.
The gold waves purled amidst the green above her;
   And a bird sang. With one sharp-taken breath,
By sunlit branches and unshaken flower
The immortal limbs flashed to the human lover,
   And the immortal eyes to look on death.

March 1910

250

A CHANNEL PASSAGE

The damned ship lurched and slithered. Quiet and
   quick
  My cold gorge rose; the long sea rolled; I knew
I must think hard of something, or be sick;
  And could think hard of only one thing—*you*!
You, you alone could hold my fancy ever!
  And with you memories come, sharp pain, and
   dole.
Now there's a choice—heartache or tortured liver!
  A sea-sick body, or a you-sick soul!

Do I forget you? Retchings twist and tie me,
  Old meat, good meals, brown gobbets, up I throw.
Do I remember? Acrid return and slimy,
  The sobs and slobber of a last year's woe.
And still the sick ship rolls. 'Tis hard, I tell ye,
To choose 'twixt love and nausea, heart and belly.

December 1909

VICTORY

All night the ways of Heaven were desolate,
   Long roads across a gleaming empty sky.
   Outcast and doomed and driven, you and I,
Alone, serene beyond all love or hate,
Terror or triumph, were content to wait,
   We, silent and all-knowing. Suddenly
   Swept through the heaven low-crouching from on
      high,
One horseman, downward to the earth's low gate.

Oh, perfect from the ultimate height of living,
   Lightly we turned, through wet woods
      blossom-hung,
Into the open. Down the supernal roads,
   With plumes a-tossing, purple flags far flung,
Rank upon rank, unbridled, unforgiving,
   Thundered the black battalions of the Gods.

DAY AND NIGHT

Through my heart's palace Thoughts unnumbered
    throng;
  And there, most quiet and, as a child, most wise,
High-throned you sit, and gracious. All day long
  Great Hopes gold-armoured, jester Fantasies,
  And pilgrim Dreams, and little beggar Sighs,
Bow to your benediction, go their way
  And the grave jewelled courtier Memories
Worship and love and tend you, all the day.

But, when I sleep, and all my thoughts go straying,
  When the high session of the day is ended,
And darkness comes; then, with the waning light,
  By lilied maidens on your way attended,
Proud from the wonted throne, superbly swaying,
  You, like a queen, pass out into the night.

POEMS 1911—1914

GRANTCHESTER

THE OLD VICARAGE,
GRANTCHESTER

(Café des Westens, Berlin, May 1912)

Just now the lilac is in bloom,
All before my little room;
And in my flower-beds, I think,
Smile the carnation and the pink;
And down the borders, well I know,
The poppy and the pansy blow . . .
Oh! there the chestnuts, summer through,
Beside the river make for you
A tunnel of green gloom, and sleep
Deeply above; and green and deep
The stream mysterious glides beneath,
Green as a dream and deep as death.
—Oh, damn! I know it! and I know
How the May fields all golden show,
And when the day is young and sweet,
Gild gloriously the bare feet
That run to bathe . . .
                    Du lieber Gott!

Here am I, sweating, sick, and hot,
And there the shadowed waters fresh
Lean up to embrace the naked flesh.
Temperamentvoll German Jews
Drink beer around;—and *there* the dews
Are soft beneath a morn of gold.
Here tulips bloom as they are told;

Unkempt about those hedges blows
An English unofficial rose;
And there the unregulated sun
Slopes down to rest when day is done,
And wakes a vague unpunctual star,
A slippered Hesper; and there are
Meads towards Haslingfield and Coton
Where *das Betreten*'s not *verboten*.

εἴθε γενοίμην . . . would I were
In Grantchester, in Grantchester!—
Some, it may be, can get in touch
With Nature there, or Earth, or such.
And clever modern men have seen
A Faun a-peeping through the green,
And felt the Classics were not dead,
To glimpse a Naiad's reedy head,
Or hear the Goat-foot piping low: . . .
But these are things I do not know.
I only know that you may lie
Day-long and watch the Cambridge sky,
And, flower-lulled in sleepy grass,
Hear the cool lapse of hours pass,
Until the centuries blend and blur
In Grantchester, in Grantchester. . . .
Still in the dawnlit waters cool
His ghostly Lordship swims his pool,
And tries the strokes, essays the tricks,
Long learnt on Hellespont, or Styx.
Dan Chaucer hears his river still
Chatter beneath a phantom mill.
Tennyson notes, with studious eye,

How Cambridge waters hurry by . . .
And in that garden, black and white,
Creep whispers through the grass all night;
And spectral dance, before the dawn,
A hundred Vicars down the lawn;
Curates, long dust, will come and go
On lissom, clerical, printless toe;
And oft between the boughs is seen
The sly shade of a Rural Dean . . .
Till, at a shiver in the skies,
Vanishing with Satanic cries,
The prim ecclesiastic rout
Leaves but a startled sleeper-out,
Grey heavens, the first bird's drowsy calls,
The falling house that never falls.

God! I will pack, and take a train,
And get me to England once again!
For England's the one land, I know,
Where men with Splendid Hearts may go;
And Cambridgeshire, of all England,
The shire for Men who Understand;
And of *that* district I prefer
The lovely hamlet Grantchester.
For Cambridge people rarely smile,
Being urban, squat, and packed with guile;
And Royston men in the far South
Are black and fierce and strange of mouth;
At Over they fling oaths at one,
And worse than oaths at Trumpington,

And Ditton girls are mean and dirty,
And there's none in Harston under thirty,
And folks in Shelford and those parts
Have twisted lips and twisted hearts,
And Barton men make Cockney rhymes,
And Coton's full of nameless crimes,
And things are done you'd not believe
At Madingley, on Christmas Eve.
Strong men have run for miles and miles,
When one from Cherry Hinton smiles;
Strong men have blanched, and shot their
    wives,
Rather than send them to St. Ives;
Strong men have cried like babes, bydam,
To hear what happened at Babraham.
But Grantchester! ah, Grantchester!
There's peace and holy quiet there,
Great clouds along pacific skies,
And men and women with straight eyes,
Lithe children lovelier than a dream,
A bosky wood, a slumbrous stream,
And little kindly winds that creep
Round twilight corners, half asleep.
In Grantchester their skins are white;
They bathe by day, they bathe by night;
The women there do all they ought;
The men observe the Rules of Thought.
They love the Good; they worship Truth;
They laugh uproariously in youth;
(And when they get to feeling old,
They up and shoot themselves, I'm told) . . .

Ah God! to see the branches stir
Across the moon at Grantchester!
To smell the thrilling-sweet and rotten
Unforgettable, unforgotten
River-smell, and hear the breeze
Sobbing in the little trees.
Say, do the elm-clumps greatly stand
Still guardians of that holy land?
The chestnuts shade, in reverend dream,
The yet unacademic stream?
Is dawn a secret shy and cold
Anadyomene, silver-gold?
And sunset still a golden sea
From Haslingfield to Madingley?
And after, ere the night is born,
Do hares come out about the corn?
Oh, is the water sweet and cool,
Gentle and brown, above the pool?
And laughs the immortal river still
Under the mill, under the mill?
Say, is there Beauty yet to find?
And Certainty? and Quiet kind?
Deep meadows yet, for to forget
The lies, and truths, and pain? . . . oh! yet
Stands the Church clock at ten to three?
And is there honey still for tea?

OTHER POEMS

BEAUTY AND BEAUTY

When Beauty and Beauty meet
   All naked, fair to fair,
The earth is crying-sweet,
   And scattering-bright the air,
Eddying, dizzying, closing round,
   With soft and drunken laughter;
Veiling all that may befall
   After—after—

Where Beauty and Beauty met,
   Earth's still a-tremble there,
And winds are scented yet,
   And memory-soft the air,
Bosoming, folding glints of light,
   And shreds of shadowy laughter;
Not the tears that fill the years
   After—after—

1912

SONG

All suddenly the wind comes soft,
   And Spring is here again;
And the hawthorn quickens with buds of green,
   And my heart with buds of pain.

My heart all Winter lay so numb,
   The earth so dead and frore,
That I never thought the Spring would come,
   Or my heart wake any more.

But Winter's broken and earth has woken,
   And the small birds cry again;
And the hawthorn hedge puts forth its buds,
   And my heart puts forth its pain.

1912

MARY AND GABRIEL

Young Mary, loitering once her garden way,
Felt a warm splendour grow in the April day,
As wine that blushes water through. And soon,
Out of the gold air of the afternoon,
One knelt before her: hair he had, or fire,
Bound back above his ears with golden wire,
Baring the eager marble of his face.
Not man's nor woman's was the immortal grace
Rounding the limbs beneath that robe of white,
And lighting the proud eyes with changeless light,
Incurious. Calm as his wings, and fair,
That presence filled the garden.

                          She stood there,
Saying, 'What would you, Sir?'

                             He told his word,
'Blessed art thou of women!' Half she heard,
Hands folded and face bowed, half long had known,
The message of that clear and holy tone,
That fluttered hot sweet sobs about her heart;
Such serene tidings moved such human smart.
Her breath came quick as little flakes of snow.
Her hands crept up her breast. She did but know
It was not hers. She felt a trembling stir
Within her body, a will too strong for her
That held and filled and mastered all. With eyes
Closed, and a thousand soft short broken sighs,
She gave submission; fearful, meek, and glad. . . .

She wished to speak. Under her breasts she had
Such multitudinous burnings, to and fro,
And throbs not understood; she did not know
If they were hurt or joy for her; but only
That she was grown strange to herself, half lonely,
All wonderful, filled full of pains to come
And thoughts she dare not think, swift thoughts and
   dumb,
Human, and quaint, her own, yet very far,
Divine, dear, terrible, familiar . . .
Her heart was faint for telling; to relate
Her limbs' sweet treachery, her strange high estate,
Over and over, whispering, half revealing,
Weeping; and so find kindness to her healing.
'Twixt tears and laughter, panic hurrying her,
She raised her eyes to that fair messenger.
He knelt unmoved, immortal; with his eyes
Gazing beyond her, calm to the calm skies;
Radiant, untroubled in his wisdom, kind.
His sheaf of lilies stirred not in the wind.
How would she, pitiful with mortality,
Try the wide peace of that felicity
With ripples of her perplexed shaken heart,
And hints of human ecstasy, human smart,
And whispers of the lonely weight she bore,
And how her womb within was hers no more
And at length hers?

        Being tired, she bowed her head
And said, 'So be it!'

        The great wings were spread,

Showering glory on the fields, and fire.
The whole air, singing, bore him up, and higher,
Unswerving, unreluctant. Soon he shone
A gold speck in the gold skies; then was gone.

The air was colder, and grey. She stood alone.

Autumn 1912

UNFORTUNATE

Heart, you are restless as a paper scrap
   That's tossed down dusty pavements by the wind;
   Saying, 'She is most wise, patient and kind.
Between the small hands folded in her lap
Surely a shamed head may bow down at length,
   And find forgiveness where the shadows stir
About her lips, and wisdom in her strength,
   Peace in her peace. Come to her, come to her!' . . .

She will not care. She'll smile to see me come,
   So that I think all Heaven in flower to fold me.
   She'll give me all I ask, kiss me and hold me,
      And open wide upon that holy air
The gates of peace, and take my tiredness home,
      Kinder than God. But, heart, she will not care.

1912

THE BUSY HEART

Now that we've done our best and worst, and parted,
  I would fill my mind with thoughts that will not
    rend.
(O heart, I do not dare go empty-hearted)
  I'll think of Love in books, Love without end;
Women with child, content; and old men sleeping;
  And wet strong ploughlands, scarred for certain
    grain;
And babes that weep, and so forget their weeping;
  And the young heavens, forgetful after rain;
And evening hush, broken by homing wings;
  And Song's nobility, and Wisdom holy,
That live, we dead. I would think of a thousand
    things,
  Lovely and durable, and taste them slowly,
One after one, like tasting a sweet food.
I have need to busy my heart with quietude.

1913

LOVE

Love is a breach in the walls, a broken gate,
 Where that comes in that shall not go again;
Love sells the proud heart's citadel to Fate.
  They have known shame, who love unloved. Even
   then
When two mouths, thirsty each for each, find slaking,
 And agony's forgot, and hushed the crying
Of credulous hearts, in heaven—such are but taking
  Their own poor dreams within their arms, and
   lying
Each in his lonely night, each with a ghost.
  Some share that night. But they know, love grows
   colder,
Grows false and dull, that was sweet lies at most.
  Astonishment is no more in hand or shoulder,
But darkens, and dies out from kiss to kiss.
All this is love; and all love is but this.

1913

274

THE CHILTERNS

Your hands, my dear, adorable,
   Your lips of tenderness
—Oh, I've loved you faithfully and well,
   Three years, or a bit less.
   It wasn't a success.

Thank God, that's done! and I'll take the road,
   Quit of my youth and you,
The Roman road to Wendover
   By Tring and Lilley Hoo,
   As a free man may do.

For youth goes over, the joys that fly
   The tears that follow fast;
And the dirtiest things we do must lie
   Forgotten at the last;
   Even Love goes past.

What's left behind I shall not find,
   The splendour and the pain;
The splash of sun, the shouting wind,
   And the brave sting of rain,
   I may not meet again.

But the years, that take the best away,
   Give something in the end;
And a better friend than love have they,
   For none to mar or mend,
   That have themselves to friend.

I shall desire and I shall find
   The best of my desires;
The autumn road, the mellow wind
   That soothes the darkening shires,
   And laughter, and inn-fires.

White mist about the black hedgerows,
   The slumbering Midland plain,
The silence where the clover grows,
   And the dead leaves in the lane,
   Certainly, these remain.

And I shall find some girl perhaps,
   And a better one than you,
With eyes as wise, but kindlier,
   And lips as soft, but true.
   And I daresay she will do.

1913

HOME

I came back late and tired last night
    Into my little room,
To the long chair and the firelight
    And comfortable gloom.

But as I entered softly in
    I saw a woman there,
The line of neck and cheek and chin,
    The darkness of her hair,
The form of one I did not know
    Sitting in my chair.

I stood a moment fierce and still,
    Watching her neck and hair.
I made a step to her; and saw
    That there was no one there.

It was some trick of the firelight
    That made me see her there.
It was a chance of shade and light
    And the cushion in the chair.

Oh, all you happy over the earth,
    That night, how could I sleep?
I lay and watched the lonely gloom;
    And watched the moonlight creep
From wall to basin, round the room.
    All night I could not sleep.

1913

THE NIGHT JOURNEY

Hands and lit faces eddy to a line;
  The dazed last minutes click; the clamour dies.
Beyond the great-swung arc o' the roof, divine,
  Night, smoky-scarv'd, with thousand coloured eyes

Glares the imperious mystery of the way.
  Thirsty for dark, you feel the long-limbed train
Throb, stretch, thrill motion, slide, pull out and sway,
  Strain for the far, pause, draw to strength again. . . .

As a man, caught by some great hour, will rise,
  Slow-limbed, to meet the light or find his love;
And, breathing long, with staring sightless eyes,
  Hands out, head back, agape and silent, move

Sure as a flood, smooth as a vast wind blowing;
  And, gathering power and purpose as he goes,
Unstumbling, unreluctant, strong, unknowing,
  Borne by a will not his, that lifts, that grows,

Sweep out to darkness, triumphing in his goal,
  Out of the fire, out of the little room. . . .
—There is an end appointed, O my soul!
  Crimson and green the signals burn; the gloom

Is hung with steam's far-blowing livid streamers.
  Lost into God, as lights in light, we fly,
Grown one with will, end-drunken huddled dreamers.
  The white lights roar. The sounds of the world die

And lips and laughter are forgotten things.
  Speed sharpens; grows. Into the night, and on,
The strength and splendour of our purpose swings.
  The lamps fade; and the stars. We are alone.

1913

THE WAY THAT LOVERS USE

The way that lovers use is this;
　　They bow, catch hands, with never a word,
And their lips meet, and they do kiss,
　　—So I have heard.

They queerly find some healing so,
　　And strange attainment in the touch;
There is a secret lovers know,
　　—I have read as much.

And theirs no longer joy nor smart,
　　Changing or ending, night or day;
But mouth to mouth, and heart on heart,
　　—So lovers say.

1913

THE FUNERAL OF YOUTH:
THRENODY

The day that *Youth* had died,
There came to his grave-side,
In decent mourning, from the county's ends,
Those scatter'd friends
Who had liv'd the boon companions of his prime,
And laugh'd with him and sung with him and wasted,
In feast and wine and many-crown'd carouse,
The days and nights and dawnings of the time
When *Youth* kept open house,
Nor left untasted
Aught of his high emprise and ventures dear,
No quest of his unshar'd—
All these, with loitering feet and sad head bar'd,
Follow'd their old friend's bier.
Folly went first,
With muffled bells and coxcomb still revers'd;
And after trod the bearers, hat in hand—
Laughter, most hoarse, and Captain *Pride* with tann'd
And martial face all grim, and fussy *Joy*,
Who had to catch a train, and *Lust*, poor, snivelling
  boy;
These bore the dear departed.
Behind them, broken-hearted,
Came *Grief*, so noisy a widow, that all said,
'Had he but wed
Her elder sister *Sorrow*, in her stead!'

And by her, trying to soothe her all the time,
The fatherless children, *Colour*, *Tune*, and *Rhyme*
(The sweet lad *Rhyme*), ran all-uncomprehending.
Then, at the way's sad ending,
Round the raw grave they stay'd. Old *Wisdom* read,
In mumbling tone, the Service for the Dead.
There stood *Romance*,
The furrowing tears had mark'd her rougèd cheek;
Poor old *Conceit*, his wonder unassuag'd;
Dead *Innocency's* daughter, *Ignorance*;
And shabby, ill-dress'd *Generosity*;
And *Argument*, too full of woe to speak;
Passion, grown portly, something middle-aged;
And *Friendship*—not a minute older, she;
Impatience, ever taking out his watch;
Faith, who was deaf, and had to lean, to catch
Old *Wisdom's* endless drone.
Beauty was there,
Pale in her black; dry-ey'd; she stood alone.
Poor maz'd *Imagination*; *Fancy* wild;
Ardour, the sunlight on his greying hair;
Contentment, who had known *Youth* as a child
And never seen him since. And *Spring* came too,
Dancing over the tombs, and brought him flowers—
She did not stay for long.
And *Truth*, and *Grace*, and all the merry crew,
The laughing *Winds* and *Rivers*, and lithe *Hours*;

And *Hope*, the dewy-ey'd; and sorrowing *Song*;—
Yes, with much woe and mourning general,
At dead *Youth's* funeral,
Even these were met once more together, all,
Who erst the fair and living *Youth* did know;
All, except only *Love*. *Love* had died long ago.

1913

THE SOUTH SEAS

MUTABILITY

They say there's a high windless world and strange,
   Out of the wash of days and temporal tide,
   Where Faith and Good, Wisdom and Truth abide,
Æterna corpora, subject to no change.
There the sure suns of these pale shadows move;
   There stand the immortal ensigns of our war;
   Our melting flesh fixed Beauty there, a star,
And perishing hearts, imperishable Love. . . .

Dear, we know only that we sigh, kiss, smile;
   Each kiss lasts but the kissing; and grief goes over;
   Love has no habitation but the heart.
Poor straws! on the dark flood we catch awhile,
   Cling, and are borne into the night apart.
   The laugh dies with the lips, 'Love' with the lover.

SOUTH KENSINGTON — MAKAWELI, 1913

CLOUDS

Down the blue night the unending columns press
  In noiseless tumult, break and wave and flow,
  Now tread the far South, or lift rounds of snow
Up to the white moon's hidden loveliness.
Some pause in their grave wandering comradeless,
  And turn with profound gesture vague and slow,
  As who would pray good for the world, but know
Their benediction empty as they bless.

They say that the Dead die not, but remain
  Near to the rich heirs of their grief and mirth.
     I think they ride the calm mid-heaven, as these,
In wise majestic melancholy train,
    And watch the moon, and the still-raging seas,
  And men, coming and going on the earth.

THE PACIFIC, *October* 1913

SONNET

(*Suggested by some of the Proceedings of the
Society for Psychical Research*)

Not with vain tears, when we're beyond the sun,
  We'll beat on the substantial doors, nor tread
  Those dusty high-roads of the aimless dead
Plaintive for Earth; but rather turn and run
Down some close-covered by-way of the air,
  Some low sweet alley between wind and wind,
  Stoop under faint gleams, thread the shadows, find
Some whispering ghost-forgotten nook, and there

Spend in pure converse our eternal day;
  Think each in each, immediately wise;
Learn all we lacked before; hear, know, and say
  What this tumultuous body now denies;
And feel, who have laid our groping hands away;
  And see, no longer blinded by our eyes.

1913

289

A MEMORY

(*From a sonnet-sequence*)

Somewhile before the dawn I rose, and stept
   Softly along the dim way to your room,
   And found you sleeping in the quiet gloom,
And holiness about you as you slept.
I knelt there; till your waking fingers crept
   About my head, and held it. I had rest
   Unhoped this side of Heaven, beneath your breast.
I knelt a long time, still; nor even wept.

It was great wrong you did me; and for gain
Of that poor moment's kindliness, and ease,
And sleepy mother-comfort!
                    Child, you know
How easily love leaps out to dreams like these,
Who has seen them true. And love that's wakened so
Takes all too long to lay asleep again.

WAIKIKI, *October* 1913

ONE DAY

To-day I have been happy. All the day
   I held the memory of you, and wove
Its laughter with the dancing light o' the spray,
   And sowed the sky with tiny clouds of love,
And sent you following the white waves of sea,
   And crowned your head with fancies, nothing
      worth,
Stray buds from that old dust of misery,
   Being glad with a new foolish quiet mirth.

So lightly I played with those dark memories,
Just as a child, beneath the summer skies,
   Plays hour by hour with a strange shining stone,
For which (he knows not) towns were fire of old,
   And love has been betrayed, and murder done,
And great kings turned to a little bitter mould.

THE PACIFIC, *October* 1913

WAIKIKI

Warm perfumes like a breath from vine and tree
   Drift down the darkness. Plangent, hidden from
     eyes,
   Somewhere an *eukaleli* thrills and cries
And stabs with pain the night's brown savagery;
And dark scents whisper; and dim waves creep to me,
   Gleam like a woman's hair, stretch out, and rise;
    And new stars burn into the ancient skies,
 Over the murmurous soft Hawaiian sea.

And I recall, lose, grasp, forget again,
   And still remember, a tale I have heard, or known,
An empty tale, of idleness and pain,
   Of two that loved—or did not love—and one
Whose perplexed heart did evil, foolishly,
A long while since, and by some other sea.

WAIKIKI, 1913

HAUNTINGS

In the grey tumult of these after-years
  Oft silence falls; the incessant wranglers part;
And less-than-echoes of remembered tears
  Hush all the loud confusion of the heart;
And a shade, through the toss'd ranks of mirth and
    crying,
  Hungers, and pains, and each dull passionate
    mood,—
Quite lost, and all but all forgot, undying,
  Comes back the ecstasy of your quietude.

So a poor ghost, beside his misty streams,
Is haunted by strange doubts, evasive dreams,
  Hints of a pre-Lethean life, of men,
Stars, rocks, and flesh, things unintelligible,
  And light on waving grass, he knows not when,
And feet that ran, but where, he cannot tell.

THE PACIFIC, 1914

HE WONDERS WHETHER TO
PRAISE OR TO BLAME HER

I have peace to weigh your worth, now all is over,
   But if to praise or blame you, cannot say.
For, who decries the loved, decries the lover;
   Yet what man lauds the thing he's thrown away?

Be you, in truth, this dull, slight, cloudy naught,
   The more fool I, so great a fool to adore;
But if you're that high goddess once I thought,
   The more your godhead is, I lose the more.

Dear fool, pity the fool who thought you clever;
   Dear wisdom, do not mock the fool that missed
     you!
Most fair,—the blind has lost your face for ever!
   Most foul,—how could I see you while I kissed you?

So . . . the poor love of fools and blind I've proved
     you,
For, foul or lovely, 'twas a fool that loved you.

1913

DOUBTS

When she sleeps, her soul, I know,
Goes a wanderer on the air,
Wings where I may never go,
Leaves her lying, still and fair,
Waiting, empty, laid aside,
Like a dress upon a chair. . . .
This I know, and yet I know
Doubts that will not be denied.

For if the soul be not in place,
What has laid trouble in her face?
And, sits there nothing ware and wise
Behind the curtains of her eyes,
What is it, in the self's eclipse,
Shadows, soft and passingly,
About the corners of her lips,
The smile that is essential she?

And if the spirit be not there,
Why is fragrance in the hair?

1913

'Oh love is fair, and love is rare;' my dear one she
said,
'But love goes lightly over.' I bowed her foolish
head,
And kissed her hair and laughed at her. Such a child
was she;
So new to love, so true to love, and she spoke so
bitterly.

But there's wisdom in women, of more than they
have known,
And thoughts go blowing through them, are wiser
than their own,
Or how should my dear one, being ignorant and
young,
Have cried on love so bitterly, with so true a
tongue?

June 1913

FAFAÏA

Stars that seem so close and bright,
Watched by lovers through the night,
Swim in emptiness, men say,
Many a mile and year away.

And yonder star that burns so white,
May have died to dust and night
Ten, maybe, or fifteen year,
Before it shines upon my dear.

Oh! often among men below,
Heart cries out to heart, I know,
And one is dust a many years,
Child, before the other hears.

Heart from heart is all as far,
Fafaïa, as star from star.

S A A N A P U, *November* 1913

HEAVEN

Fish (fly-replete, in depth of June,
Dawdling away their wat'ry noon)
Ponder deep wisdom, dark or clear,
Each secret fishy hope or fear.
Fish say, they have their Stream and Pond;
But is there anything Beyond?
This life cannot be All, they swear,
For how unpleasant, if it were!
One may not doubt that, somehow, Good
Shall come of Water and of Mud;
And, sure, the reverent eye must see
A Purpose in Liquidity.
We darkly know, by Faith we cry,
The future is not Wholly Dry.
Mud unto mud!—Death eddies near—
Not here the appointed End, not here!
But somewhere, beyond Space and Time,
Is wetter water, slimier slime!
And there (they trust) there swimmeth One
Who swam ere rivers were begun,
Immense, of fishy form and mind,
Squamous, omnipotent, and kind;
And under that Almighty Fin,
The littlest fish may enter in.
Oh! never fly conceals a hook,
Fish say, in the Eternal Brook,
But more than mundane weeds are there,
And mud, celestially fair;

Fat caterpillars drift around,
And Paradisal grubs are found;
Unfading moths, immortal flies,
And the worm that never dies.
And in that Heaven of all their wish,
There shall be no more land, say fish.

1913

THE GREAT LOVER

I have been so great a lover: filled my days
So proudly with the splendour of Love's praise,
The pain, the calm, and the astonishment,
Desire illimitable, and still content,
And all dear names men use, to cheat despair,
For the perplexed and viewless streams that bear
Our hearts at random down the dark of life.
Now, ere the unthinking silence on that strife
Steals down, I would cheat drowsy Death so far,
My night shall be remembered for a star
That outshone all the suns of all men's days.
Shall I not crown them with immortal praise
Whom I have loved, who have given me, dared with
    me
High secrets, and in darkness knelt to see
The inenarrable godhead of delight?
Love is a flame:—we have beaconed the world's night.
A city:—and we have built it, these and I.
An emperor:—we have taught the world to die.
So, for their sakes I loved, ere I go hence,
And the high cause of Love's magnificence,
And to keep loyalties young, I'll write those names
Golden for ever, eagles, crying flames,
And set them as a banner, that men may know,
To dare the generations, burn, and blow
Out on the wind of Time, shining and streaming. . . .

These I have loved:
               White plates and cups, clean-gleaming,
Ringed with blue lines; and feathery, faery dust;
Wet roofs, beneath the lamp-light; the strong crusts
Of friendly bread; and many-tasting food;
Rainbows; and the blue bitter smoke of wood;
And radiant raindrops couching in cool flowers;
And flowers themselves, that sway through sunny
     hours,
Dreaming of moths that drink them under the moon;
Then, the cool kindliness of sheets, that soon
Smooth away trouble; and the rough male kiss
Of blankets; grainy wood; live hair that is
Shining and free; blue-massing clouds; the keen
Unpassioned beauty of a great machine;
The benison of hot water; furs to touch;
The good smell of old clothes; and others such—
The comfortable smell of friendly fingers,
Hair's fragrance, and the musty reek that lingers
About dead leaves and last year's ferns. . . .
                                    Dear names,
And thousand other throng to me! Royal flames;
Sweet water's dimpling laugh from tap or spring;
Holes in the ground; and voices that do sing;
Voices in laughter, too; and body's pain,
Soon turned to peace; and the deep-panting train;
Firm sands; the little dulling edge of foam
That browns and dwindles as the wave goes home;
And washen stones, gay for an hour; the cold
Graveness of iron; moist black earthen mould,

Sleep; and high places; footprints in the dew;
And oaks; and brown horse-chestnuts, glossy-new;
And new-peeled sticks; and shining pools on grass;—
All these have been my loves. And these shall pass,
Whatever passes not, in the great hour,
Nor all my passion, all my prayers, have power
To hold them with me through the gate of Death.
They'll play deserter, turn with the traitor breath,
Break the high bond we made, and sell Love's trust
And sacramented covenant to the dust.
——Oh, never a doubt but, somewhere, I shall wake,
And give what's left of love again, and make
New friends, now strangers. . . .
                              But the best I've known
Stays here, and changes, breaks, grows old, is blown
About the winds of the world, and fades from brains
Of living men, and dies.
                              Nothing remains.

O dear my loves, O faithless, once again
This one last gift I give: that after men
Shall know, and later lovers, far-removed,
Praise you, 'All these were lovely'; say, 'He loved.'

MATAIEA, 1914

RETROSPECT

In your arms was still delight,
Quiet as a street at night;
And thoughts of you, I do remember,
Were green leaves in a darkened chamber,
Were dark clouds in a moonless sky.
Love, in you, went passing by,
Penetrative, remote, and rare,
Like a bird in the wide air,
And, as the bird, it left no trace
In the heaven of your face.
In your stupidity I found
The sweet hush after a sweet sound.
All about you was the light
That dims the greying end of night;
Desire was the unrisen sun,
Joy the day not yet begun,
With tree whispering to tree,
Without wind, quietly.
Wisdom slept within your hair,
And Long-Suffering was there,
And, in the flowing of your dress,
Undiscerning Tenderness.
And when you thought, it seemed to me,
Infinitely, and like a sea,
About the slight world you had known
Your vast unconsciousness was thrown. . . .

O haven without wave or tide!
Silence, in which all songs have died!
Holy book, where hearts are still!
And home at length under the hill!
O mother-quiet, breasts of peace,
  Where love itself would faint and cease
O infinite deep I never knew,
I would come back, come back to you,
Find you, as a pool unstirred,
Kneel down by you, and never a word,
Lay my head, and nothing said,
In your hands, ungarlanded;
And a long watch you would keep;
And I should sleep, and I should sleep!

MATAIEA, *January* 1914

TIARE TAHITI

Mamua, when our laughter ends,
And hearts and bodies, brown as white,
Are dust about the doors of friends,
Or scent a-blowing down the night,
Then, oh! then, the wise agree,
Comes our immortality.
Mamua, there waits a land
Hard for us to understand.
Out of time, beyond the sun,
All are one in Paradise,
You and Pupure are one,
And Taü, and the ungainly wise.
There the Eternals are, and there
The Good, the Lovely, and the True,
And Types, whose earthly copies were
The foolish broken things we knew;
There is the Face, whose ghosts we are;
The real, the never-setting Star;
And the Flower, of which we love
Faint and fading shadows here;
Never a tear, but only Grief;
Dance, but not the limbs that move;
Songs in Song shall disappear;
Instead of lovers, Love shall be;
For hearts, Immutability;
And there, on the Ideal Reef,
Thunders the Everlasting Sea!

And my laughter, and my pain,
Shall home to the Eternal Brain.
And all lovely things, they say,
Meet in Loveliness again;
Miri's laugh, Teïpo's feet,
And the hands of Matua,
Stars and sunlight there shall meet,
Coral's hues and rainbows there,
And Teūra's braided hair;
And with the starred *tiare's* white,
And white birds in the dark ravine,
And *flamboyants* ablaze at night,
And jewels, and evening's after-green,
And dawns of pearl and gold and red,
Mamua, your lovelier head!
And there'll no more be one who dreams
Under the ferns, of crumbling stuff,
Eyes of illusion, mouth that seems,
All time-entangled human love.
And you'll no longer swing and sway
Divinely down the scented shade,
Where feet to Ambulation fade,
And moons[1] are lost in endless Day.
How shall we wind these wreaths of ours,
Where there are neither heads nor flowers?

[1] Mr Iolo Williams has suggested to me, rightly, I think, that the sense here requires 'noons'. I do not like to make the alteration in the text, as 'moons' is clearly written in the manuscript. —E. M.

Oh, Heaven's Heaven!—but we'll be missing
The palms, and sunlight, and the south;
And there's an end, I think, of kissing,
When our mouths are one with Mouth. . . .

　Taü here, Mamua,
Crown the hair, and come away!
Hear the calling of the moon,
And the whispering scents that stray
About the idle warm lagoon.
Hasten, hand in human hand,
Down the dark, the flowered way,
Along the whiteness of the sand,
And in the water's soft caress,
Wash the mind of foolishness,
Mamua, until the day.
Spend the glittering moonlight there
Pursuing down the soundless deep
Limbs that gleam and shadowy hair,
Or floating lazy, half-asleep.
Dive and double and follow after,
Snare in flowers, and kiss, and call,
With lips that fade, and human laughter
And faces individual,
Well this side of Paradise! . . .
There's little comfort in the wise.

　　PAPEETE, *February* 1914

307

1914

THE TREASURE

When colour goes home into the eyes,
   And lights that shine are shut again,
With dancing girls and sweet birds' cries
   Behind the gateways of the brain;
And that no-place which gave them birth, shall
   close
The rainbow and the rose:—

Still may Time hold some golden space
   Where I'll unpack that scented store
Of song and flower and sky and face,
   And count, and touch, and turn them o'er,
Musing upon them; as a mother, who
Has watched her children all the rich day through,
Sits, quiet-handed, in the fading light,
When children sleep, ere night.

August 1914

I. PEACE

Now, God be thanked Who has matched us with His
    hour,
  And caught our youth, and wakened us from
    sleeping,
With hand made sure, clear eye, and sharpened power,
  To turn, as swimmers into cleanness leaping,
Glad from a world grown old and cold and weary,
  Leave the sick hearts that honour could not move,
And half-men, and their dirty songs and dreary,
  And all the little emptiness of love!

Oh! we, who have known shame, we have found
    release there,
  Where there's no ill, no grief, but sleep has mending.
    Naught broken save this body, lost but breath;
Nothing to shake the laughing heart's long peace there
  But only agony, and that has ending;
  And the worst friend and enemy is but Death.

II. SAFETY

Dear! of all happy in the hour, most blest
    He who has found our hid security,
Assured in the dark tides of the world that rest,
    And heard our word, 'Who is so safe as we?'
We have found safety with all things undying,
    The winds, and morning, tears of men and mirth,
The deep night, and birds singing, and clouds flying,
    And sleep, and freedom, and the autumnal earth.
We have built a house that is not for Time's throwing.
    We have gained a peace unshaken by pain for ever.
War knows no power. Safe shall be my going,
    Secretly armed against all death's endeavour;
Safe though all safety's lost; safe where men fall;
And if these poor limbs die, safest of all.

III. THE DEAD

Blow out, you bugles, over the rich Dead!
 There's none of these so lonely and poor of old,
 But, dying, has made us rarer gifts than gold.
These laid the world away; poured out the red
Sweet wine of youth; gave up the years to be
 Of work and joy, and that unhoped serene,
 That men call age; and those who would have been,
Their sons, they gave, their immortality.

Blow, bugles, blow! They brought us, for our dearth,
 Holiness, lacked so long, and Love, and Pain.
Honour has come back, as a king, to earth,
 And paid his subjects with a royal wage;
And Nobleness walks in our ways again;
 And we have come into our heritage.

IV. THE DEAD

These hearts were woven of human joys and cares,
    Washed marvellously with sorrow, swift to mirth.
The years had given them kindness. Dawn was theirs,
    And sunset, and the colours of the earth.
These had seen movement, and heard music; known
    Slumber and waking; loved; gone proudly
      friended;
Felt the quick stir of wonder; sat alone;
    Touched flowers and furs and cheeks. All this is
    ended.

There are waters blown by changing winds to
    laughter
And lit by the rich skies, all day. And after,
    Frost, with a gesture, stays the waves that dance
And wandering loveliness. He leaves a white
    Unbroken glory, a gathered radiance,
A width, a shining peace, under the night.

V. THE SOLDIER

If I should die, think only this of me:
  That there's some corner of a foreign field
That is for ever England. There shall be
  In that rich earth a richer dust concealed;
A dust whom England bore, shaped, made aware,
  Gave, once, her flowers to love, her ways to roam,
A body of England's, breathing English air,
  Washed by the rivers, blest by suns of home.

And think, this heart, all evil shed away,
  A pulse in the eternal mind, no less
    Gives somewhere back the thoughts by England
      given;
Her sights and sounds; dreams happy as her day;
  And laughter, learnt of friends; and gentleness,
    In hearts at peace, under an English heaven.

APPENDIX

FRAGMENT

I strayed about the deck, an hour, to-night
Under a cloudy moonless sky; and peeped
In at the windows, watched my friends at table,
Or playing cards, or standing in the doorway,
Or coming out into the darkness. Still
No one could see me.

        I would have thought of them
—Heedless, within a week of battle—in pity,
Pride in their strength and in the weight and firmness
And link'd beauty of bodies, and pity that
This gay machine of splendour 'ld soon be broken,
Thought little of, pashed, scattered. . . .

        Only, always,
I could but see them—against the lamplight—pass
Like coloured shadows, thinner than filmy glass,
Slight bubbles, fainter than the wave's faint light,
That broke to phosphorus out in the night,
Perishing things and strange ghosts—soon to die
To other ghosts—this one, or that, or I.

April 1915

THE DANCE

A Song

As the Wind, and as the Wind,
   In a corner of the way,
Goes stepping, stands twirling,
Invisibly, comes whirling,
Bows before, and skips behind,
   In a grave, an endless play—

So my Heart, and so my Heart,
   Following where your feet have gone,
Stirs dust of old dreams there;
He turns a toe; he gleams there,
Treading you a dance apart.
   But you see not. You pass on.

April 1915

SONG

The way of love was thus.
He was born one winter morn
With hands delicious,
And it was well with us.

Love came our quiet way,
Lit pride in us, and died in us,
All in a winter's day.
There is no more to say.

1913 (?)

SOMETIMES EVEN NOW...

Sometimes even now I may
Steal a prisoner's holiday,
Slip, when all is worst, the bands,
  Hurry back, and duck beneath
Time's old tyrannous groping hands,
  Speed away with laughing breath
Back to all I'll never know,
Back to you, a year ago.

Truant there from Time and Pain,
What I had, I find again:
Sunlight in the boughs above,
  Sunlight in your hair and dress,
The Hands too proud for all but Love,
  The Lips of utter kindliness,
The Heart of bravery swift and clean
  Where the best was safe, I knew,
And laughter in the gold and green,
  And song, and friends, and ever you
With smiling and familiar eyes,
  You—but friendly: you—but true.

And Innocence accounted wise,
  And Faith the fool, the pitiable.
Love so rare, one would swear
  All of earth for ever well—
Careless lips and flying hair,
  And little things I may not tell.

It does but double the heart-ache
When I wake, when I wake.

1912 (?)

SONNET: IN TIME OF REVOLT

The Thing must End. I am no boy! I AM
  No BOY!! being twenty-one. Uncle, you make
  A great mistake, a very great mistake,
In chiding me for letting slip a 'Damn!'
What's more, you called me 'Mother's one ewe lamb,'
  Bade me 'refrain from swearing—for *her* sake—
  Till I'm grown up' ... —By God! I think you take
Too much upon you, Uncle William!

You say I am your brother's only son.
I know it. And, 'What of it?' I reply.
My heart's resolved. *Something must be done.*
So shall I curb, so baffle, so suppress
This too avuncular officiousness,
Intolerable consanguinity.

January 1908

322

A LETTER TO A LIVE POET

Sir, since the last Elizabethan died,
Or, rather, that more Paradisal muse,
Blind with much light, passed to the light more
  glorious
Or deeper blindness, no man's hand, as thine,
Has, on the world's most noblest chord of song,
Struck certain magic strains. Ears satiate
With the clamorous, timorous whisperings of to-day,
Thrilled to perceive once more the spacious voice
And serene utterance of old. We heard
—With rapturous breath half-held, as a dreamer
  dreams
Who dares not know it dreaming, lest he wake—
The odorous, amorous style of poetry,
The melancholy knocking of those lines,
The long, low soughing of pentameters,
—Or the sharp of rhyme as a bird's cry—
And the innumerable truant polysyllables
Multitudinously twittering like a bee.
Fulfilled our hearts were with that music then,
And all the evenings sighed it to the dawn,
And all the lovers heard it from all the trees.
All of the accents upon all the norms!
—And ah! the stress on the penultimate!
We never knew blank verse could have such feet.

Where is it now? Oh, more than ever, now
I sometimes think no poetry is read
Save where some sepultured Cæsura bled,
Royally incarnadining all the line.
Is the imperial iamb laid to rest,
And the young trochee, having done enough?
Ah! turn again! Sing so to us, who are sick
Of seeming-simple rhymes, bizarre emotions,
Decked in the simple verses of the day,
Infinite meaning in a little gloom,
Irregular thoughts in stanzas regular,
Modern despair in antique metres, myths
Incomprehensible at evening,
And symbols that mean nothing in the dawn.
The slow lines swell. The new style sighs. The Celt
Moans round with many voices.
                                    God! to see
Gaunt anapæsts stand up out of the verse,
Combative accents, stress where no stress should be,
Spondee on spondee, iamb on choriamb,
The thrill of all the tribrachs in the world,
And all the vowels rising to the E!
To hear the blessed mutter of those verbs,
Conjunctions passionate toward each other's arms,
And epithets like amaranthine lovers
Stretching luxuriously to the stars,
All prouder pronouns than the dawn, and all
The thunder of the trumpets of the noun!

January 1911

FRAGMENT ON PAINTERS

There is an evil which that Race attaints
Who represent God's World with oily paints,
Who mock the Universe, so rare and sweet,
With spots of colour on a canvas sheet,
Defile the Lovely and insult the Good
By scrawling upon little bits of wood.
They'd snare the moon, and catch the immortal sun
With madder brown and pale vermilion,
Entrap an English evening's magic hush . . .

THE TRUE BEATITUDE
(*BOUTS-RIMÉS*)

They say, when the Great Prompter's hand shall ring
   Down the last curtain upon earth and sea,
   All the Good Mimes will have eternity
To praise their Author, worship love and sing;
Or to the walls of Heaven wandering
   Look down on those damned for a fretful d——,
   Mock them (all theologians agree
On this reward for virtue), laugh, and fling

New sulphur on the sin-incarnadined . . .
   Ah, Love! still temporal, and still atmospheric,
     Teleologically unperturbed,
We share a peace by no divine divined,
   An earthly garden hidden from any cleric,
     Untrodden of God, by no Eternal curbed.

1913

SONNET REVERSED

Hand trembling towards hand; the amazing lights
Of heart and eye. They stood on supreme heights.

Ah, the delirious weeks of honeymoon!
  Soon they returned, and, after strange adventures,
Settled at Balham by the end of June.
  Their money was in Can. Pacs. B. Debentures,
And in Antofagastas. Still he went
  Cityward daily; still she did abide
At home. And both were really quite content
  With work and social pleasures. Then they died
They left three children (besides George, who drank):
  The eldest Jane, who married Mr Bell,
William, the head-clerk in the County Bank,
  And Henry, a stock-broker, doing well.

LULWORTH, 1 *January* 1911

IT'S NOT GOING TO HAPPEN
AGAIN

I have known the most dear that is granted us here,
  More supreme than the gods know above,
Like a star I was hurled through the sweet of the
    world,
  And the height and the light of it, Love.
I have risen to the uttermost Heaven of Joy,
  I have sunk to the sheer Hell of Pain—
But—it's not going to happen again, my boy,
  It's not going to happen again.

It's the very first word that poor Juliet heard
  From her Romeo over the Styx;
And the Roman will tell Cleopatra in hell
  When she starts her immortal old tricks;
What Paris was tellin' for good-bye to Helen
  When he bundled her into the train—
Oh, it's not going to happen again, old girl,
  It's not going to happen again.

CHATEAU LAKE LOUISE
CANADA, 1913

THE LITTLE DOG'S DAY

All in the town were still asleep,
When the sun came up with a shout and a leap.
In the lonely streets unseen by man,
A little dog danced. And the day began.

All his life he'd been good, as far as he could,
And the poor little beast had done all that he should.
But this morning he swore, by Odin and Thor
And the Canine Valhalla—he'd stand it no more!

So his prayer he got granted—to do just what he
    wanted,
Prevented by none, for the space of one day.
'*Jam incipiebo,*[1] *sedere facebo,*'[2]
In dog-Latin he quoth, '*Euge! sophos! hurray!*'

He fought with the he-dogs, and winked at the she-
    dogs,
A thing that had never been *heard* of before.
'For the stigma of gluttony, I care not a button!' he
Cried, and ate all he could swallow—and more.

He took sinewy lumps from the shins of old frumps,
And mangled the errand-boys—when he could get
    'em.
He shammed furious *rabies,*[3] and bit all the babies,[3]
And followed the cats up the trees, and then ate 'em!

[1] Now we're off.   [2] *I'll* make them sit up.
[3] Pronounce either to suit rhyme.

329

They thought 'twas the devil was holding a revel,
And sent for the parson to drive him away;
For the town never knew such a hullabaloo
As that little dog raised—till the end of that day.

When the blood-red sun had gone burning down,
And the lights were lit in the little town,
Outside, in the gloom of the twilight grey,
The little dog died when he'd had his day.

July 1907

332